Can You Cope with Happiness?

Joyce Duco

edited by
Janey P. Jones

Can You Cope with Happiness?

Joyce Duco
BNA Corporate Center
Building 200, Suite 207
Nashville, TN. 37217

Library of Congress Catalog Card Number 83-91233

Second Printing - February 1984
Third Printing - October 1984

ISBN 0-9612896-0-0

Printed by
Curley Printing Company
411 Cowan Street
Nashville, TN. 37207
United States of America

Contents

Preface

Happiness should be a way of life, not a once-in-a-while experience. However, many of us were taught false values and feel guilty about having the best life has to offer.

Before we can experience the "good life" our self-image must be equal to it and able to accept it (free of guilt). This book teaches proper attitudes about happiness, success, money and good health and it teaches how we can use our amazing mind to attract these conditions. It is a spiritual, scientific, and practical approach to daily living.

Joyce Duco

ABOUT THE AUTHOR

As Sister Fabian in the Order of the Sisters of St. Joseph in New Orleans, Louisiana, I taught in the parochial schools for twenty-one years. My last year as a nun (1969) was spent as a probation officer at the Juvenile Court in the City of New Orleans. It was a year of tremendous emotional stress.

I was actually leading a double life. During the week, from 9:00 to 5:00, I was Joyce Duco, probation officer, and at night and on weekends I reassumed my role as Sister Fabian. As Joyce Duco I wore street clothes for the first time in twenty-one years and found people responding to me as a person rather than a religious symbol. Men kidded with me, offered me cigarettes and asked me out after work. The religious community knew I was working as a probation officer and only the judge at the Juvenile Court knew I was Sister Fabian in street clothes.

Since I was the only nun in my local religious community not teaching, and my work as a probation officer was unfamiliar to the other sisters, communication in the religious community became difficult. A series of illnesses and surgeries which had begun in 1964 continued to sap my strength. I had responsibility of caring for my father who was critically ill and died a few months before I left the convent. I had become a very confused and totally exhausted human being faced with overwhelming adjustments when I finally decided to take a leave of absence from the convent.

But after leaving the convent I found that I was still Sister Fabian to family and friends. . .and I began to realize I would have to leave New Orleans in order to learn about Joyce Duco. . .

So I moved to Las Vegas where no one knew anything about me except that my name was Joyce Duco and I was from New Orleans!

My first job was working nights at the Dunes Hotel where I monitored the counting in the cage. There I learned the meaning of culture shock! After a few months at the Dunes I was hired as a medical assistant to one of the physicians in Vegas. Unfortunately my sickness followed me there. I received Emergency

Room treatment shortly after I arrived, for physical exhaustion and hypoglycemia due to anxiety and stress. The following year I required surgical treatment for an unrelated illness.

After 18 months in Las Vegas I moved to Denver - still searching for my niche, for direction in a career, and still getting sick and having surgery. When I could no longer adjust to the tempo of office work I experimented with sales. Being a Mary Kay beauty consultant was a catalyst for discovering my niche. In sales my time was my own and I was able to attend sales meetings and lectures on positive thinking.

My life began to turn around in 1974 when I attended a seminar that made me realize that most of my problems (mental, physical, financial) were caused by MY ATTITUDE about my health and my financial condition. The speaker said, "Illness can be psycosomatic." This made me sit up and listen.

For ten years physicians had been telling me my poor health was "psychosomatic" or my "nerves" - yet they continued to remove tumors from my body. During this time I found their remarks offensive, an insult to my intelligence. Had I understood the proper meaning of the term "psychosomatic" I would have understood the part my attitude (my mind) played in my illnesses and made an effort to discipline my thinking to put an end to my trips to the hospital.

> Webster defines psychosomatic as:
> "designating or of a physical disorder of the body originating in or aggravated by the psychic or emotional processes of the individual."

A familiar example is the stomach ulcer. An ulcer is a sore in the stomach usually caused by negative emotions like worry or stress. Negative thinking causes negative chemical reactions in the body. The immune system weakens and we become ill.

I decided to attend the seminar on mind development to learn about psychosomatic illness. When I began to understand how emotional stress affects the physical body, I decided that if my mind could cause my illness, my mind could also PREVENT illness. . .I decided I would use the power of my mind, but in a positive way to insure health, rather than in the negative way that had surely insured illness. Instead of psychosomatic illness, I would opt for PSYCHOSOMATIC HEALTH, by repeating, "I am healthy".

I became acutely aware of my thoughts and began to discipline them. I rejected thoughts that depressed me and focused on pleasant thoughts. I rejected thoughts of privation by saying over and over again, "I am rich" - and I said it with all the conviction I could muster!

After reading Claude Bristol's book, *The Magic of Believing,* I formed the habit of looking into the mirror daily, standing tall and full of faith and enthusiasm, and saying to my reflection, "I am happy, healthy and prosperous." I almost weakened in the beginning and told myself, "You're anything but happy, healthy and prosperous. You're miserable, sick and broke!" But I had learned and truly believed that my subconscious mind had attracted negative conditions to me because I EXPECTED THEM. I had learned and truly believed that my subconscious mind was programmed by the way I thought and spoke day after day. I knew that I would turn my life around by changing my thinking habits and persisted in a mental diet of often repeated positive thoughts. As a result of this disciplined positive attitude, the yearly trips to the hospital ended and I began to be the joyful, prosperous individual God intended me to be.

Soon others began to notice the favorable changes in my life and I was asked by the founder of Mind Development, Inc. to teach the seminars I had been attending.

Since 1975 I have been conducting my own seminars, lectures and workshops on how to develop a positive mental attitiude by understanding the power of thought in order to attract health, happiness and prosperity. This book is for you, to educate you about your great potential. Read it carefully, practice its principles faithfully, and it will greatly improve your quality of living.

Joyce Duco

For information concerning seminars,
lectures, tapes contact:
Joyce Duco
BNA Corporate Center
Building 200, Suite 207
Nashville, TN. 37217
(615) 366-0455

CHAPTER I

Our Amazing Mind

Much is being written these days about the power of the mind. We are fascinated to hear that yogis sleep on nails and walk on hot coals without scarring their bodies; that little old ladies lift cars to save their grandchildren; that some psychics can move objects with their minds; that people are being taught to levitate; that the terminally ill can heal themselves. What is this mysterious power? And who possesses it?

We all do!

When Jesus said to those observing Him perform the miracles, "You can do this. . .and greater. . ." He meant exactly that! The power of the mind is the God-power within each of us, and our link-up with this infinite intelligence and wisdom is the subconscious mind.

The Subconscious Mind

While we are relaxing, meditating, or sleeping, our minds operate on the different subconscious levels of Alpha, Delta, and Theta. At these subconscious levels we conserve energy, receive creative ideas, experience ESP, do problem-solving and transcend the limitations of time and space.

It is no coincidence that those who meditate regularly retain their youthful appearance. Not only do we rejuvenate body and mind while "tuning in" frequently to the subconscious, but it is at these subconscious levels (Alpha, Delta, Theta) that we receive solutions to problems and answers to questions. Answers do not come to us in times of anxious thought or frenzied activity, but only in moments of calm when we let our thoughts go worry free. At this time the mind "switches channels" from the conscious level (Beta) to the subconscious level of Alpha where we are in tune with infinite wisdom and intelligence, and good ideas, answers and solutions come easily to us.

The Subconscious Operates Like a Computer

I like to compare the subconscious mind to a computer. Computers are programmed. We are programmed. We are programmed by our parents, our bosses, our teachers, our peers, spouses, religious teachers, commercials, news media. . .Any suggestive influence in our lives programs our subconscious to some degree. It has been estimated that 80 - 85% of our daily conditioning (programming) is negative. If we are AWARE of these influences and the control they can have over our actions and decisions, we can guard against any negative or destructive tendencies. Just remember, IF YOU ARE NOT IN CONTROL, SOMEONE OR SOMETHING ELSE IS. I want my own values system in my computer, not someone else's!

The Subconscious Works with Repetition

We program our subconscious with our repetitious thinking and speaking. How often do we repeat, "That burns me up." "I hate this." "She gives a pain in the neck". (or elsewhere) "That kills me". And so on. . .

Don't be surprised if you actually feel uncomfortable in the presence of those people who "give you a pain, burn you up," etc.

And how often do you think, "I can't do it." "I'll never make it." Don't be surprised then, when you don't succeed. YOU ARE PROGRAMMING YOURSELF TO FAIL.

Our everyday thinking is a form of self-hypnosis. Each time we repeat a word or thought we are sending our subconscious a blueprint to work from.

To Change Your Life, Change Your Thinking

How can we change our lives? By changing our programming - our repetitious thinking. Tell yourself, "I CAN do this." "I AM attractive." "I AM successful." Tell yourself often, many times a day, and say it WITH ENTHUSIASM.

As mentioned earlier, several years back sickness had become a way of life for me. The more I thought surgery, the more surgery I had. The more I thought depression, the more depressed I became. When I learned that the subconscious works with repetition that was when I made a conscious effort to eliminate sickness, depression and privation from my thoughts and my vocabulary and replaced them with thoughts of health, happiness and prosperity. Just as we pull a weed from the garden and plant a flower, we can replace a negative trait by repeating positive statements. Remember, the subconscious mind works with repetition and what we keep repeating to ourselves, ABOUT ourselves, we become.

The September 1979 issue of *Time* magazine carried an article entitled, "Little Black Box". A department store on the East Coast used this Little Black Box experimentally for nine months and saved $600,000 in shoplifting costs during that period of time. The Little Black Box is "basically a sound mixer like those used by disco dejays. The Box mingles blank music with subliminal anti-theft messages, 'I am honest - I will not steal'. These messages are repeated rapidly, 9,000 times an hour, at a very low volume barely audible to shoppers and employees. But they do register in some deep recess of the brain and apparently influence behavior." This is only one example of how the subconscious responds to REPETITIOUS SUGGESTION.

The Subconscious - Our "Genie"

Like any other computer, the subconscious works only on the information provided to it - good, bad, indifferent. . .It has no mind of its own and cannot select or edit material. We program our subconscious through repetition, visualization and emotion. The subconscious does what we or some other programmer commands - without struggle or effort, without question, without judgement. The subconscious knows only to obey. I like to refer to the subconscious as my genie because it obeys all my commands. But I must be selective. I must decide what is most beneficial to me and program accordingly. THE SUB-CONSCIOUS DOES NOT EDIT!

The Subconscious Aids Recuperation

Before my third surgery I told my doctor I hoped it wouldn't be as unpleasant as my first two. After surgery I had not been able to get out of bed until the third day, couldn't eat, couldn't focus my eyes, couldn't have visitors. He said he'd see what he could do to make my recuperation more comfortable.

After that third operation I returned to my room resting comfortably. I ate, I could see. I even had visitors (and enjoyed them) that first night. But the best part was that I felt happy and peaceful. I felt that even if the tumor had been malignant I could have accepted it with a peaceful mind. I simply felt happy and was very curious about this new and strange experience.

When my doctor came for his routine visit the next day I told him how good I felt and finally asked him what he had done that was different. He smiled and said, "I spoke to you in the recovery room and I said to your subconscious that you would feel well, happy and have no problems." I said, "Don't snap your fingers because it's working!"

I mentioned this experience in one of my recent seminars and a nurse who was attending said it reminded her of one of the doctors at the hospital where she worked. This particular doctor is called "Whispering Sam" because he whispers positive suggestions to his patients about their prognosis and recovery in the recovery room. The nurse said that his patients had fewer problems than any of the other patients. Hopefully the day will come when it will be standard procedure to play tapes with positive suggestions about health and happiness to patients in all recovery rooms.

The Conscious Mind

Joseph Murphy says in the *Power of Your Subconscious Mind,* "Your conscious mind is the dynamo that awakens the power of your subconscious."

The conscious mind is sometimes referred to as the Beta level. At this level we perceive information through our five senses. This limits us to the five average ways to obtain information - seeing, hearing, touching, smelling and tasting. However, to learn to transcend this conscious level and to go within, is to tune into unlimited universal knowledge.

A the conscious (Beta) level we reason and make decisions logically. The subconscious mind does not use logic. It does not reason. Once your decisions, goals, fears are sent to the subconscious, it can only obey. It cannot decide what is good or bad for you. It simply obeys the command you send it from your conscious mind via repetition, visualization and feeling.

The Conscious Mind Must Be Disciplined

One approach to disciplining the conscious mind is to begin viewing and judging situations with our intellect and not with our emotions. So often we control or are controlled by feelings of guilt. This is so easy to do because most of us have been conditioned to guilt from early childhood. Feeling guilty has become second nature to us. Because guilt is an emotion and the subconscious is programmed by emotion, we must prevent this negative feeling from being transmitted to the subconscious. If we do permit feelings of guilt to reach our subconscious we are likely to attract punishment in the form of sickness, accident or disappointment.

To view situations intelligently instead of emotionally is to come in touch with truth. If someone is trying to put a guilt trip on you, back off and look at the situation and the facts. Ask yourself, "Am I truly guilty, or is he/she trying to control me by making me FEEL guilty?" Also ask yourself, "Does my self image encourage feelings of guilt?" Remember, guilt is a powerful weapon that is often used by those who wish to be in control. View the facts intelligently before permitting a feeling of guilt to filter into the subconscious.

In Summary

To become the happy, healthy, prosperous beings we are meant to be, we must function effectively at both the conscious and the subconscious levels - and we all can learn to do this with practice. We must understand the power of thought and discipline our thinking. Our conscious mind can learn to sift information and logically decide upon goals and aspirations to program into the subconscious. Our conscious mind must be the disciplinarian. We must consciously decide what goes into the subconscious. Positive programming will produce a positive lifestyle and vice versa. The subconscious can only obey - can only work with the information it receives. As soon as the subconscious receives the information the conscious mind sends, it goes to work to make it happen - good or bad.

CHAPTER II

Universal Laws
How They Affect Us

All aspects of our universe are governed by laws. This is the way Universal Order is maintained. There is the law of gravity, the law of electricity, the law of relativity, etc. Man is part of the universe and man is also governed by certain laws. The law that governs the mind of man is the Law of the Mind which is the law of attraction - like attracts like. WHAT YOU THINK ABOUT, YOU BRING ABOUT.

Fear Attracts the Thing Feared

Perhaps you have never heard the law expressed in exactly this way. Nevertheless, you've experienced the result, or the consequences of using this law improperly. Have you known people who feared falling down steps? They are the ones who fall down steps. What about mothers who fear their children will be hurt or become ill? Those children are usually sickly and accident prone. If you are afraid of being robbed, you probably will be. This is how the Law of the Mind works to our disadvantage. The fears in our consciousness become manifest in our experience. What we think about, we bring about. Job in the Old Testament said, "The things I have feared the most have come upon me." What he thought about, he brought about. Fear is an emotion and the subconscious is programmed by emotion.

Universal Laws Operate for Everyone - No Exceptions

Let us consider for a moment the law of electricity. If I want toast bread, I plug in the toaster, I put in the bread and I get toast. But, if I plug in my finger, I am electrocuted. The law of electricity does not stop operating because I don't know that such a law exists. The law of electricity does not stop working because I don't understand how it works. . .it keeps flowing through the wires. The electric current does not cut off and wait for me to learn about the law. My ignorance of the law does not save me. The law of electricity is no respector of persons. It performs the same way for the rich, the poor, the good or the evil person.

Watch a child bouncing a ball. He throws it straight up into the air and looks up to see where it will fall. We all know that if the child doesn't move, the ball will fall on his head. We also know the law of gravity won't suspend the ball in space until the child learns that what goes up must come down, and that he must move out of the way to avoid getting hit on the head. The law of gravity continues to operate the way it was created to operate, and if the child doesn't move, he'll learn something about the law through the unpleasant experience of being hit. The law of gravity works the same for a child as it does for one who understands this law.

Most of us have experienced the 'bump on the head' and learned about the Law of the Mind the hard way. Often we attract negative experiences because we are ignorant of the Law of the Mind and its attraction properties. Now that we know about the Law of the Mind let us use this law to our advantage and attract positive experiences rather than pain and disappointment. Let us begin to use the law wisely and always remember that what we think about we will surely bring about.

Choose Thoughts Carefully

You can't plant tomato seeds and grow cucumbers. If you think thoughts of sickness (as I did) you will not attract good health. If you want to become rich, think rich. If you want to become successful, think success. If you want to become attractive, think attractive; thin, think thin. Your mind is like a magnet. You will become a magnet for what you are thinking about. But remember, you must FEEL it. The subconscious mind is also programmed with EMOTION. Discipline yourself and sincerely believe that you DESERVE the good you desire.

The Law of Life

Christ taught another unchangeable law - the law of life. That is, "As you sow, so shall you reap." I KNOW all of us have experienced this law at work in our lives. We have all gotten back what we have given - good or bad. God created balance in this universe. When you do good, you receive good in return from someone, some day. If you do an injustice, the same applies.

While I was in Miami recently preparing for a seminar, I was literally "taken for a ride." The "ride" should have taken fifteen minutes and cost $6.00 but took thirty-five minutes and cost $15.00. It aggravated me that I was "taken" but after I communicated my feelings and got control, I blessed the deceitful cab-driver and the situation and declared some good would come from it. That evening a young man who had heard me on radio earlier that day stopped by my hotel to purchase a complete set of my tapes. Interestingly enough, he was a former cab-driver. You see, the universe "owed" me one and gave me back twice the amount I was cheated out of. The universe also "owes" the cab-driver one, and somewhere, sometime, some injustice will be done him in retribution for his unfairness to me!

"As you sow, so shall you reap" - an unchangeable law of the universe. And not knowing about the law or understanding it does not stop it from affecting us. It keeps operating despite our ignorance of and/or disbelief in it.

At one time I was charging $15.00 an hour for private sessions with individuals. After a telephone conference with a woman out of state I suggested that she send me only $10.00 instead of the usual $15.00 since she had long distance charges. Two weeks passed and no check. During this time I had had another client hand me a check and say, "Joyce, I hope you won't be offended but I've enjoyed this session so much that I'd like to pay you $25.00. I received my just payment from another source at another time. God's laws will insure rewards or punishments according to our just deserts. We get out of life exactly what we put into it. Maybe this is what God meant when He said, "Revenge is Mine". His laws which are constantly operating will take care of all injustices.

Children and the Laws

Some public school systems teach death, and that is fine. Since death is inevitable we should form positive and fearless attitudes about it. But what system has ever taught LIFE?

We teach books, not children - and we rarely touch on the subject of attitudes. We're afraid that if we deviate too much from our subject matter we won't complete all the material asigned to us to cover!

If we would teach about the Law of Life and the Law of the Mind we could mold the minds in our charge each year with correct thinking and healthy attitudes and thus produce happy, confident citizens who respect each other.

In Summary

When Christ said, "Be in the world but not of it," I believe He was telling us not to get caught up into the negative values we've been victims of - the race consciousness of lack of self-worth, inferiority, hatred, that we have to "struggle to achieve", etc. Let us not be OF THIS WORLD of negative beliefs, for that will surely draw negative situations to us. Instead, "let us put on the mind of Christ," as St. Paul admonishes us. Let us think as Christ did-believing that God is an all-good, all-loving, totally just Father Who can only will GOOD FOR US. And let us know that this all-good God has set the laws of the universe in motion for us to use correctly in order to become happy, healthy, prosperous beings.

CHAPTER III

SELF-HYPNOSIS

In hypnosis a subject reaches the subconscious level of consciousness assisted by the hypnotist's relaxation techniques. During these sessions information long forgotten by the conscious mind can be recalled and experiences from early childhood can be retrieved from the deep recesses of the subconscious mind. At these subconcious levels suggestions can be made to help the subject be rid of undesirable habits.

In self-hypnosis we can learn to relax and reach these levels of the subconscious without the aid of the hypnotist. We, too, can make suggestions to ourselves to rid ourselves of unwanted habits. (See chapters on Meditation and Visualization.) This is called self-hypnosis. We are constantly making suggestions to ourselves - both positive and negative. OUR EVERYDAY THINKING IS A FORM OF SELF—HYPNOSIS. We can use self-hypnosis in a positive way to support development of a positive mental attitude and attract good into our lives.

Key to Successful Self-Hypnosis

In order for self-hypnosis to be effective, the subject must earnestly desire, BOTH ON A CONSCIOUS AND SUBCONSCIOUS LEVEL, to be free of an undesirable habit. Otherwise the suggestions are blocked by the not-yet-convinced subconscious and the bad habit continues. However, when the conscious mind and the subconscious mind are in complete accord, the bad habit ceases.

Necessity of Motivation

Desire motivates us to achieve. If we lack this motivation, we'll have to depend on will-power alone to succeed. . .and that is always a struggle. When we have a REASON to put an end to an undesirable habit, the task is easier than when we lack the motivation and must struggle along using only will-power to do what we really don't want to do in the first place.

A friend of mine had tried unsuccessfully many times to stop smoking. One day while driving to a business appointment the wind blew live ashes from her cigarette onto her expensive new outfit and ruined it. She threw the cigarette out the window and hasn't smoked since. She was motivated!

Sometimes when the conscious mind and the subconscious mind are not ready to release the undesirable habit and will-power alone is used, strange side effects occur.

A lady in one of my seminars said she had recently married and had told her new husband that if he loved her enough, he'd stop smoking. Of course the new bridegroom wanted to prove his love and stopped smoking. However, he broke out in a rash all over his body! Obviously, he was not ready, or motivated, (on both conscious and subconscious levels) to give up his cigarettes, and his struggle with will-power was manifesting itself as a rash.

"X" Out the Candy Habit

Assuming you have an honest desire to stop eating chocolate candy because it keeps you overweight, you are ready for self-hypnosis. Find a quiet place, take a comfortable position, close your eyes and relax. When you feel you've reached the Alpha level (See chapter on Meditation) visualize a screen before you like a motion picture screen. See a piece of chocolate candy on this screen with a large black "X" across the candy. Now suggest to yourself that the next time you have a desire to eat chocolate candy all you have to do is take a deep breath and drink some water and your desire to eat chocolate will vanish. Of course drinking water and taking a deep breath are simply trigger mechanisms for your subconscious to work with to overcome your inordinate desire for sweets. When you drink water and breathe deeply your subconscious gets the message and goes to work to help you lose your desire for chocolate candy because you've programmed it, using self-hypnosis, with the suggestion, "The next time I have a desire to eat chocolate candy, all I have to do is take a deep breath and drink some water and my desire to eat chocolate will vanish." If you feel that you drink alcoholic drinks excessively or would like to stop smoking, use the same technique with the 'X" across the bottle or the package of cigarettes.

Because this is a new technique to you, your mind will require practice. Meditate and see the "X" across the candy, bottle or cigarettes for at least 21 days. Once the program is in your subconscious, your "genie" will go to work obediently to carry out your command.

Self-Hypnosis to Control Overeating

Sometimes the body wants to overeat when the mind knows we've had enough. Since the mind is more powerful than the body we can use self-hypnosis to help the body accept what the mind knows is best for it.

In my undisciplined days when I went to buffets I was overwhelmed by the variety of foods I had to chose from and would often overeat. I developed and now use the following self-hypnosis visualization technique before leaving for a party or social event where I might be tempted to "pig out."

I sit, relax and quiet my mind and sink into Alpha. Then I visualize myself at the party looking at the delicious, attractive assortment of food. I see myself making wise, nutritious choices and taking only conservative portions. Then I visualize myself enjoying every mouthful and happy and pleased that I chose only enough to be satisfied and comfortable. I use my mind to prepare my body to desire only certain foods in moderate servings. Then when I get to the buffet I am not overwhelmed and my appetite is completely satisfied with the choices I make. Often the body wants more than it needs or should have. I use this technique to successfully SYNCHRONIZE MIND AND BODY, conscious mind and subconscious mind with my intelligent desires.

Cassette Tapes Aid Self-Hypnosis

Cassette tapes can be a very effective tool to aid self-hypnosis. You can make your own tapes using affirmations to attract whatever you want in life - financial increase, improved relationships, a better job, excellent health, the right companion, spouse, etc. Begin with five or six affirmations on a thirty-minute tape. Repeat the affirmations over and over until the end of the tape. Play it when you go to bed so that your subconscious can receive the suggestions while you sleep. Also play the tape when you get up in the morning, while dressing or driving to work or at quiet times during the day so that your conscious mind benefits from the repetition. Do this for at least twenty-one days. The repetition on a conscious and subconscious level will help you create a new consciousness, a new way of thinking. Every few weeks change or add to the affirmations on the tape according to your needs or desires. With these new programs in your "computer" you'll soon notice the good you'll begin to attract.

Sample Affirmations

I am happy, healthy and rich because as a child of God I deserve to be. I am not dependent upon persons or conditions for my abundance, for God is my source.

My monthly income is $_____. With my $_____ monthly income I enjoy the good things in life and am able to make wise financial investments.

My subconscious mind now frees me from all resentment, all anger, all bitterness, all ideas of punishment towards anyone and everyone. I am free to see only good in myself and others.

I go about my life in peace and tranquility.

My subconscious mind now accepts _____ pounds as my true weight and my subconscious mind directs me to foods and activities that keep me at my true weight of _____.

I am protected from all physical, mental and spiritual harm at all times. Wherever I am, God is, and all is well.

I have perfect 20/20 vision. I can see clearly, up close and at a distance.

Excellent health, happiness and financial success are now a way of life for me.

The relationship between _____ and me is now supported with love, harmony and wisdom.

CHAPTER IV

Meditation

Meditation is not just for gurus, nuns, priests, ministers or yogis. It is a viable, practical way for all of us to bring order and balance into our lives. We live in a fast-paced and stressful society, but we can learn to take quiet control by "going within".

The Need to Meditate

What does meditation do for us? Meditation provides time for our minds and bodies to relax - it "recharges our batteries". When we stop in the middle of a busy day to relax and meditate, the cells of our bodies are rejuvenated and we receive the energy we need to continue at peak performance.

Meditation retards the aging process. When we're relaxed we conserve energy. When we are nervous, rushing around or under stress, we dissipate energy.

I like to think of meditation as a planned meeting with myself when I can relax, sort out priorities, discover my goals and visualize them, and get in touch with or receive creative ideas.

Meditation Breaks or Coffee Breaks?

Some corporations are now giving their employees the choice of a coffee or a meditation break. For those who choose a meditation break, a quiet restful room is provided where they can relax mentally and physically for a few moments, morning and afternoon. These corporations are starting to realize that employees who meditate regularly are easier to get along with, more productive and better able to cope with stressful situations on the job.

Meditation takes practice and discipline, but once you make it a part of your daily schedule, you'll look forward to it and thoroughly enjoy that meeting with yourself.

Meditation Technique

I teach a meditation technique that I'd like to share with you. If you are already using another one and it works for you, keep using it. Use whatever is most effective for you.

First of all, try to set aside the same time every day for your relaxation/meditation time - about five to fifteen minutes. If you know you will meditate at a certain time each day it will help prepare your mind and body so that you can experience maximum benefits for time spent.

Wear loose clothing, find a quiet place and take a comfortable position. You may want to sit up or lie down. Whatever position you take, be sure your spine is straight so that the energy can flow. Do not cross legs or arms.

Close your eyes and take three or four deep breaths through your nose. Hold the breath as long as you can before exhaling through the nose. As you exhale, feel your whole body relaxing from your toes to your head. Begin counting slowing from 10 to 1. Visualize each number as you are counting.

Then see yourself in your favorite place of relaxation - on a beach, in the mountains, wherever you feel relaxed. You might even see yourself floating on a cloud. . . .

Or you might visualize yourself in a luxurious house, beautifully decorated to your taste. Settle into a comfortable chair, look around the room and enjoy every detail of your new surroundings. Imagination is free, so create your dream house and put yourself in it!

If you are a nature lover, see yourself surrounded by natural beauty. . .a meadow filled with wildflowers, a quiet forest, a hidden lake where the deer come to drink at sunset . . .

Your favorite place might be a room with a gorgeous view overlooking the ocean. There you'll feel refreshed by sunlight streaming through the sliding glass doors that fill one side of the

room and by the sound of the surf pounding on the rocks below.
. .

Experience in your mind whatever appeals to you. Experience it fully - smell the tangy salty smell of the ocean and see the sunlight sparkle as it dances on the waves. . .Or rest in the lush, sunny meadow and enjoy the vibrant colors of the wildflowers. . .

Recalling your favorite place of relaxation can be a welcome respite during a stressful day or after a particularly trying activity. You can be in your favorite place of relaxation anytime you like and in a matter of seconds. No one can deprive you of this secret place. It is yours . . .your own private haven where you go to relax mind and body and restore your spirit.

Now that you are relaxed and in the meditative state from breathing deeply, counting down from 10 to 1, and from seeing yourself in your favorite place of relaxation, you may want to use this relaxation time to pray, to simply rest quietly to relieve mind and body stress, to ask questions and receive answers, or to visualize your goals. (See chapter on Visualization)

As you practice relaxation and meditation you will find yourself going more and more quickly into the meditative (Alpha) state. You may find that a simple countdown or a few deep breaths are all that are necessary.

Don't spend all your time asking questions in meditation. Take time to listen for answers, too. Don't be disappointed if you don't receive your answer during one meditation. Just stay receptive and you will receive it at another time when you're relaxed. It may come to you while you are reading a newspaper or magazine, while talking to a friend, or even while exercising or watching TV. You may have a dream that will give you your answer. Tune in. Take time to listen. You'll know you have your answer when you get that sudden flash of inspiration or intuition. . .when something "clicks" for you. Enjoy moments of quiet while driving, getting ready for work, eating alone. Stop filling your world with distractions and begin to develop your mental and spiritual powers.

Children and Meditation.

Children who know how to relax are more productive in school and less hyperactive. Being relaxed also helps to get better grades on tests. Nothing comes through when we're uptight or worried during an exam, no matter how well prepared we are. But when we relax, we unblock the chanels through which all knowledge flows, and the answers will come.

Rewards of Meditation

Those who regularly practice the discipline of relaxation and meditation know how to release physical tension and mental stress and concentrate attention on what is truly important to them. Relaxation is the key to success, to achieving goals and solving problems, to gaining information we need for problems we are working on. Relaxation is also the key to good health.

Our extrasensory perception is heightened as a result of meditation. As we learn to consciously dismiss troubled worrisome thinking, our minds become fine-tuned to situations and people and we can make clear decisions, correct judgements and enjoy quality living.

CHAPTER V

Vizualization -
What You See Is What You Get!

We can all visualize because we have all been given the gift of imagination. Imagination and visualization are much the same, but random imagination - daydreaming - differs from visualization as a discipline. Disciplined visualization coupled with emotion and repeated over and over will enable you to attract your goal. You can visualize yourself as that person who possesses the traits you desire, or who has the financial success, athletic ability, etc., that you want to achieve.

Many athletes use visualization to improve their athletic skills. According to the June 1978 issue of *Sky* magazine, "Jack Nicklaus uses it with every shot. He asks for a club. He grips the club, stands behind the ball and looks toward the green, seemingly in a trance. What he is doing in this trance is imagining the shot." And according to this article he's been doing it for years.

Richard Suin, a psychologist at Colorado State University, developed an imagery program called Visual Motor Behavior Rehearsal in 1970 and used it successfully with the U.S. Ski Team. Then Barbara Kolonay, a student at Hunter College in New York, borrowed Suinn's technique and applied it to free-throw shooting with basketball players. She suggested to the players that they sit in a straight-backed chair, relax, close their eyes, then imagine the exact details: going to the free throw line, being handed the ball, hearing the crowd, feeling the weakness in their body, breathing heavily, shooting the free throw and seeing it go through the basket. This visualization and relaxation technique was done in fifteen ten-minute sessions during the last half of the basketball season. As a result, the team improved from 67.3 to 69.2 percent.

Preparation for Visualization

To prepare for visualization, use the meditation techniques suggested in the chapter on meditation: deep breaths, counting backwards and visualizing the number from 10 down to 1, seeing yourself in your favorite place of relaxation. When you feel comfortable and completely at ease in this mental environment, create a screen and make it large enough to project images of yourself achieving your goals. Then begin to visualize and FEEL yourself as that person who possesses the traits you desire - that person who has the financial success, physical beauty, athletic ability, etc., that you want to achieve.

Visualizing Weight Loss

Do you want to lose weight? Visualize yourself thin. Get a picture of an attractive, thin person and put it on your refrigerator or anywhere you can see it often. Visualize yourself stepping on the scales and see the indicator stop at your desired weight. . .Feel your clothes fit loosely on your thinning body. Visualize your friends congratulating you on losing "all that weight!". . .Imagine yourself shopping for a new wardrobe for your smaller figure. Experience a sense of accomplishment as the salesgirl compliments you on your slender, attractive figure. . .Do this twice a day. Your subconscious needs to receive its new blueprint REPEATEDLY. The new "thin person blueprint" will gradually replace the old "fat person blueprint" in your subconscious and before long (and without apparent effort) you will begin to lose your desire for foods that cause you to gain weight. The pounds will drop away and the new THIN you will become a reality.

And if you don't lose weight stop and ask yourself, "Do I really WANT to be thin? Am I REALLY READY for the RESPONSIBILITY of being attractive?" You may say you want to lose weight but you may have a secret reason why you won't or don't. One overweight friend who had tried countless diets and couldn't seem to take off the excess poundage finally admitted to me that she was afraid that if she lost weight she'd cheat on her husband!

You can break any undesirable habit you WANT to - when you're READY. You must have a desire and reason to do it. The desire motivates you to achieve your goal and when you're truly motivated you won't have to struggle with will-power.

Visualize Material Goals

When I first learned about the power of the mind and what visualization could do, I decided to visualize for a Monte Carlo. Twice a day I would relax, visualize myself opening the door of my new, sky-blue Monte Carlo. . .In my imagination I felt contentment as I settled into the driver's seat. . .grasped the steering wheel, adjusted the rearview mirror and turned on the ignition. . I could actually SMELL the new interior and hear the clear stereo. After using this visualization for several days I was given the name of a man who used the skin care product I was selling. This man was the manager of a chevrolet company. I called on him and after getting his order our conversation turned to the power of the mind. He invited me to lecture to their staff later in the week. After the lecture we chatted a bit in his office and he asked if I ever made business trips out of town. I said I did. He said, "The next time you go out of town on a business trip stop by and use one of our Monte Carlos!" I did.

At another sales lecture I gave I noticed the door prize was a loaf of home-made bread which is a weakness of mine. While the members were discussing their business part of the meeting I sat quietly, almost hidden behind the podium, closed my eyes, took a few deep breaths and began visualizing the M.C. handing me the door prize. After the lecture my name was drawn and the M.C. handed me the bread. . .What you see is what you get!

One of my students from Los Angeles, wrote to tell me how she and a friend used visualization to achieve a financial goal. Her friend was in debt for $125,000 but did not want to declare bankruptcy because he wanted to pay his debtors. They began visualizing a check for $150,000 to cover everything. The week she wrote me her friend had received a $70,000 commission and was expecting a $100,000 commission the following week from the sale of mining properties.

Can Visualization Influence Time?

In September, 1975, I was notified by ABC that another network would air the movie, *The Weekend Nun,* before the end of that year. (This movie was a Paramount Production and was originally aired in 1972 by the ABC network. It was based on my experiences as a Nun and probation officer during my last year in the convent.) I was anxious for it to be shown before December when everyone becomes involved in Christmas parties and shopping. In meditation I began to visualize the words "*Weekend Nun* by November, 1975". I called the local TV station to check with their programming department about their September, October and November schedules, but the *Weekend Nun* was not yet scheduled. However, during the first week of November a friend from ABC in New York called to say that an updated movie schedule had just been released for November. The *Weekend Nun* was aired on November 17, 1975.

Overcoming Fears and Financial Difficulties

If you are having difficulty making ends meet financially, stop saying, "I won't have enough money to pay all my bills this month." Instead, see yourself sitting at your desk, preparing to pay all your bills and hear yourself say, "I have plenty of money to pay my bills." And say it with enthusiasm. Visualize yourself contentedly writing out each check with the amount you owe until every bill is paid. Feel grateful that you are able to pay all your bills and have plenty left over. And always, PUT AS MUCH FEELING AS POSSIBLE into your visualization. FEEL it and BELIEVE it will be done.

If you've just applied for a job that you want, don't say, "I know they won't choose me for this job." Instead, take time out, relax and visualize someone from the company calling you and telling you you have the job. Then see yourself happy and grateful for the news. See it, feel it and believe. Try it. If it works for athletes and terminal illness, it can work for you!

Do you have a fear of flying? Picture and feel yourself getting on the plane with enthusiasm, enjoying a pleasant conversation with the passenger next to you. Or see yourself totally relaxed in you seat, enjoying some quiet time thinking or reading during the flight. Then see yourself getting off the plane, safe and happy.

Are you afraid the teacher will call on you and you won't know the answer? Visualize your teacher asking a question and see yourself raising your hand to volunteer the answer. Then see yourself stand and answer the question correctly. See that happy, satisfied expression on your face that comes when you've shown the rest of the class how smart you are. This repeated imagery of self-confidence will replace the image you have of yourself as a person who LACKS self-confidence.

Using the mind to achieve goals and overcome fears takes practice, effort, discipline. But the rewards are limitless. YOU CAN DO ANYTHING YOU WANT TO DO.

What You See Is What You Get

Visualization or imaging is a most effective way of providing your subconscious with an exact blueprint to work from. Because of this, see your goals in exact details as to size, amount, color, texture. (See chapter on Goals.) Use the five physical senses to experience the reality of your goals in your mind. Remember the subconscious is programmed by VISUALIZATION, EMOTION, REPETITION. . .so image your goal (visualize) at least twice a day (repetition) using as much feeling and enthusiasm as you can (emotion).

Visualization and meditation go hand in hand. You must be in the meditative (Alpha) state to visualize effectively, and the ability to visualize is a powerful mental tool.

CHAPTER VI

Happiness - A Way of Life

An old proverb tells us that happiness is a journey, not a destination. Happiness should also be a way of life, not a once-in-a-while experience. But far too many of us do not view life as a happy experience. Why? Because we're confused. We don't know who we are or what we are. We have been taught conflicting theories about ourselves.

Sinners? or Children of God?

We have been taught that we are sinners and that as sinners we deserve the "cross" which manifests itself as depression, poverty, sickness, unhappy relationships, failure, etc. Some of us take this "cross" so seriously that when we're enjoying the good things in life we begin to worry and start wondering when punishment will strike. To be happy and have everything go right for a whole week is more than many of us can bear! That we "deserve evil" has been pounded so long and so hard into our consciousness that we are uncomfortable with happiness. Then when negativity does present itself again after several days of happiness we say complacently, "I knew it was too good to last."

In one breath we are told that we are sinners and in the next we are told we are children of God. Doesn't this strike you as a contradiction? How can we believe we are sinners and children of God at the same time? When you look at your infant son/daughter or grandchild, do you look lovingly at the infant in the crib and say or think, "Look at the little sinner?" Of course not! You look lovingly at the innocent baby and say, "look at the little ANGEL!"

God, an all-good, all-perfect Being CANNOT create a sinful human being. If "sin" means that I make mistakes or "miss the mark", I agree that I am a sinner, for indeed I make mistakes. But I am not a sinner in the sense that I am an evil person or was born an evil person who deserves a "sinner's lot" in life.

As children of God the universe is ours because we are heirs to our Father's kingdom. God is all-good and all-perfect. In His kingdom He creates perfection and abundance, not lack or limitation. If we don't have what we need, it is not that the supply is limited. It is OUR ABILITY TO RECEIVE THAT IS LIMITED.

If we are sick, miserable, struggling financially we are not reflecting the conditions that befit a child of God. As His children, we deserve HAPPINESS, HEALTH and PROSPERITY. Anything else is poor advertisement for the Father.

If God is all good He cannot will us to be sick or unhappy. This is a contradiction. It is impossible for God to cause evil, lack or misery in our lives if He is all good.

When we hear of a family in which the husband has lost his job, the wife is sick and the child is failing and giving trouble in school, why is it that we say, "It's God's will"? That's an insult to an all-loving Creator Who is incapable of anything but good!

God has nothing to do with this negative situation except that He PERMITS it. The husband lost his job because he lacked faith in God and in himself. The wife was distressed because she was concerned that no money was coming in. The stress caused chemical reactions in her body, her immune system broke down and she became ill. The child, confused and bombarded by the negative energy transmitted by both parents, acted out at school.

God is not CAUSING, but PERMITTING this to exist.

Whatever happened to, "If there's anthing you need, ask, believe, and I will give it to you."

The Force of Faith

Christ said, "Faith can move mountains" and I interpret this literally because I've learned how our amazing mind works. To me faith is essential to happiness. Faith removes all obstacles.

Faith CAN move mountains! When we learn to combine and develop our spiritual and mental energies we acquire whatever we need. Christ promised this. . .and those of us who use faith and discipline to develop mentally and spiritually are experiencing the fulfillment of this promise.

One afternoon while I was still teaching in the parochial schools one of the students asked me to stay and say the rosary so that our boys' team would win the championship game that afternoon. After the rosary another student asked, "Sister, how does God know who to let win? You know our competition is praying to beat us, and we're praying to beat them." It was a good question and at the time I had no answer. If that student would ask me that question today my answer would be, "The team that has the greatest faith will win." Faith works like a magnet. It attracts, sometimes "miraculously" whatever we focus on.

Faith simply means, "to believe in". An atheist can have faith. If you believe in yourself, in what you are doing, in another person or in God, you have faith. Faith is the force that transforms obstacles into opportunities.

You can have negative faith as well as positive faith. When you believe and say repeatedly, "I just know this business will fail," you are expressing BELIEF in failure. Just as positive faith is a force to attract positive results, negative faith is also a force that attracts negative results.

Faith in False Values

Sometimes we make the mistake of placing our faith in false values - false securities. For many of us "security" is someone we can depend on for our needs, or money in the bank or a good job. If that someone you depend on dies tonight where is your secruity? As for money in the bank, ask those who experienced the Great Depression what happened to their financial security overnight! And job security is a myth these days - from executives to errand boys.

What, then is security? Does it exist? How do we find it? True security comes from within. True security is knowing and believing that YOU WILL ALWAYS HAVE WHAT YOU NEED WHEN YOU NEED IT. True security is knowing that your needs will be met at all levels, physically, mentally, materially, spiritually. . .that you have and will always have peace of mind. If security to you is dependence on another person, relationship, circumstance, institution, corporation, organization, or anything else outside of yourself, you're in for a disappointment. You're looking in all the wrong places.

How Self-Image Affects Relationships

We seek happiness in relationships but sometimes find unhappiness instead. Why? There are many reasons.

Some of us expect the whole world to love us and we feel rejected if this does not happen. This CANNOT happen. The whole world didn't love Jesus Christ and HE was perfect! Why should we believe we can be pleasing to everyone? Impossible.

Some of us find a friend and try to make that person over to our liking. We have no right to impose our needs on another person or expect that friend to make us happy by being what we want him/her to be. That person has enough to do to keep himself happy! The responsibility of making two people happy is unfair and unreasonable. Each person is responsible for his own happiness. And when you've finally attained happiness, share it.

If a new relationship is a struggle, accept the fact that maybe the two of you don't have enough in common to keep it going. For one person to admit this to the other is not a rejection. That person is simply communicating those feelings and suggesting that you both stop prolonging the agony of an unhappy relationship. It doesn't mean one is better than the other. It doesn't mean that one is inferior to the other. It simply means there isn't enough in common to keep the relationship going and growing. To communicate this way shows maturity. If the other party feels rejected it's becuase he or she interprets honest communication as rejection because of low self-image. It is not intended as rejection.

No one can hurt us, reject us, make us feel guilty unless we accept these feelings. No one can touch us emotionally unless we let them. If we would view situations and people objectively and intelligently, minus emotions, we would make better judgments about others AND ourselves. If we have a healthy self-image and take an objective viewpoint, no one can make us feel rejected or guilty or hurt our feelings.

Rejection vs. Opinion

According to an article in the December, 1982 *McCalls*, "Being Turned Down Can Be A Step Up," Lee Pennington a successful author, received enough rejection slips from publishers in six months to paper four walls! BUT IT NEVER STOPPED HIM! He continued to believe in himself and he continued writing and submitting. That's self-confidence! Lee Pennington obviously viewed those rejection slips as simply opinions, not rejections.

So, too, in relationships, when we express our opinions about the other person it is not a rejection. BUT IF WE BELIEVE ABOUT OURSLEVES WHAT THAT PERSON IS TELLING US, WE ACCEPT THE REJECTION. It is our self-image that needs improvement.

Overcoming Disappointments

For some of us happiness means not being disappointed. A proper mental attitude dispels disappointment. This requires disciplined thinking and faith (believe that we deserve good). Our mind can entertain only one thought at a time and the thought we're focusing on is the thought WE CHOOSE to focus on. We can choose to mentally work through a negative experience and put it aside, then replace it with something positive. Or, we can choose to dwell on the unpleasant experience and inevitably become depressed. The choice is ours.

If you continually choose the negative thought, ask yourself why. Do you enjoy the self-pity? Do you need the punishment? Do you enjoy hating, feeling miserable? Has guilt become a way of life for you ? You must be getting something out of it or you wouldn't continue to do it!

Dealing with Negative Situations

If you are faced with an unpleasant person or situation that you can do nothing about, bless the situation. Bless the person, and KNOW and BELIEVE some good will come from it. Say, "My life is in Divine Order. Some good will come from this." Do this when you have flat tire, when your boss is angry with you, or if your home burns down. (God forbid!) Your faith will be the magnet to attract good from a seemingly negative situation and you'll seldom experience disappointment. All of us have seen good come out of disaster. . .the "blessing in disguise." When you expect good to come from negativity, it will. What you think about, you bring about.

Life is to lived, not tolerated - enjoyed, not endured. Happiness is ours when we improve our attitude about life. With a proper mental attitude we learn to take control of our lives. Nothing can depress us, reject us, control us if we discipline our thinking with thoughts of faith in God's goodness for us.

"There is no duty so much underrated as the duty
of being happy."

Robert Louis Stevenson

Happiness, Our Divine Right

As children of God we have divine rights - Happiness, Health and Prosperity. In His goodness He made earth our domicile and filled it with unlimited good and beauty for us to enjoy. He did not create a torture chamber or an arena filled with "crosses". If we have crosses, we've created them through our lack of understanding spiritual truths, and our lack of faith in His goodness and power. An all-perfect God cannot create frivolously. . .we are not His playthings. Each of us is God's perfect creation, here for a definite purpose. Through prayer and meditation we will discover our mission, our reason for being and will become enthusiastic about life and living.

Happiness is not a once-in-a-while experience. It is a way of life. It's alright to be happy. It's God's will.

CHAPTER VII

Prosperity

Prosperity means having MORE THAN ENOUGH. Prosperity means having more than enough money to pay all bills, unexpected expenses, and taxes - with plenty left over for fun and sharing. Prosperity means having more than enough friends, joy, confidence, health, beauty. Prosperity means having more than enough talent, ability, wisdom to enjoy a successful career or rewarding retirement. And prosperity means having enough time to enjoy all this good, and to share it.

We have been told that money is the root of all evil. WRONG. The LACK of it is! We're also told that the poor have a sure place in heaven and that the rich will scarcely make it. We make it sound like poverty is a virtue. If poverty is so great, who do you know that is trying to become poor!

As a Nun I took a Vow of Poverty, but I was never deprived of my needs. I never missed a meal, never worried about rent, and always had the clothes, medical care and school supplies I needed. I vowed to be DETACHED from worldly things, not deprived of them.

Christ did not preach poverty. He taught DETACHMENT, poverty of spirit.. Don't let material things possess and control you. See to it that YOU POSSESS THEM. And don't desire material possessions and money so much that you steal or cheat to acquire them. That's when money becomes the root of all evil, when you get it by offending others. But desiring and receiving money legitimately, and for legitimate reasons - to pay our debts, take care of ourselves and our families, and to enjoy the good things in life is not evil; it is good.

God is the source of all good, an inexhaustible storehouse

supplying every conceivable need, and we, his children, have access to it all. There are many channels through which this good can flow to us - jobs, gifts, refunds, stocks, customers, legacies - but these are only channels, and good only comes if and when we're ready to receive it. It truly is "the Father's good pleasure to give us the kingdom."

Jesus Christ's Prosperity Consciousness

Christ provided the best wine at the Feast of Cana. He provided food for the multitudes so they wouldn't be hungry and weak on their journey home. Christ wore one of the most expensive garments of his day, a seamless robe. The soldiers who crucified Him didn't rip it up and divide the pieces among themselves as was the custom. They recognized the robe's value, kept it whole and complete and cast lots for it. Judas was the treasurer of the group. He kept the purse and bought whatever they needed. They didn't go around in rags and they didn't go hungry. Christ didn't teach poverty or privation, he taught detachment. Poverty is no virtue, and it certainly does not befit a child of God.

Why Privation?

We are the most affluent nation in the world, yet many Americans experience privation. Why? Because some of our social programs promote the "poverty consciousness" and encourage laziness. People become irresponsible with money when they don't earn it. They lack incentive because they are secure with the knowledge that they can depend on a steady (though meager) monthly income. And, after receiving this limited income so long without effort, they learn to adjust to a lifestyle of limitation.

Some recipients have spent a lifetime TAKING. For them there is no purpose, no incentive, no challenge in life.

The children in these families see TAKING as a way of life. When they become parents they expect to be taken care of. Then the children's children expect to be taken care of. . .Now we have three generations who have never seen a parent leave every morning and go to work. They have never contributed to the society that supports them. They think the world owes them a living and if they're not GIVEN what they want, some may steal, believing it's their due.

Society's social programs deprive these victims of ever experiencing a feeling of accomplishment. Their lives are boring and unfulfilled.

We don't help the indigent by giving them money for doing nothing. We help them by training them to take care of themselves and the children they bring into this world, and by educating them to realize their potential to become useful and productive members of society. We must all do our share and contribute to our world in order to develop a prosperity consciousness and experience true prosperity.

Attitudes about Money

We hear that "the rich get richer and the poor get poorer." True. It is true because the rich THINK RICH and the poor THINK POOR. The rich think rich because they are comfortable with prosperity. The poor think poor because they are comfortable with poverty or limitation. Self-image has everything to do with these conditions.

Many of us still have a poverty consciousness because of old attitudes towards money. We have been taught that money is evil, so we fear money. At the same time we know we need money. We can't live or die without money. . .but we feel guilty for having money!

We can change all this when we begin to look at money as a blessing, not something to feel guilty about. TRUE PROSPERITY INCLUDES ENJOYING WHAT WE ALREADY HAVE. Be at peace and know that it is not His will for us to be deprived. God creates in abundance for His children. Accept this abundance and STOP FEELING GUILTY. When we learn to enjoy and accept prosperity, it becomes a permanent part of our lives.

Prosperity through Circulation of Money

Money must be circulated so that its supply does not become

limited. Hoarding limits, but circulating increases. Mary Katherine McDougall in her book *Happiness, Now* tells of a young man in an Eastern legend who was determined to break the poverty history of his family and become very rich and very wise. This young man finally succeeded in getting an audience with the wisest and wealthiest man in the kingdom and asked him the secret of his success. The old man told him: "No matter how much or how little you have, always give one-tenth to yourself and one-tenth to God" (or your source of good). The legend ends with the young man becoming very rich and very happy and wise by using the secret. Ms. McDougall goes on to explain that the young man was rich, happy and wise because he had learned to handle his money and not let his money handle him.

Importance of Tithing

Many ancient civilizations practiced tithing,- the Romans, Egyptians, Babylonians, Persians, Arabians, Greeks, Chinese. Catherine Ponder, in *Open Your Mind to Prosperity* explains that the word "tithe" means "tenth" and that the ancients felt that ten was a magic number of increase and invoked it by tithing.

If is not necessary that we tithe to a church. We should tithe (circulate money) to our source of good. If your church is your source of good, tithe to it. If a person or organization has been helpful to you and you feel that person or organization is your source of good, tithe to them.

When I was finally convinced of the importance of tithing I decided to tithe to a friend who had been supportive of my work through her prayers. As I was making out my check to tithe to her, I wondered if this was a wise move since I thought I might need that money at the end of the month to pay bills. Remembering that tithing is a universal law of prosperity I blessed the check of $50 and mailed it to her as my source of good. Two days later I received a check from a former student in New Orleans who was tithing to me.

It is essential that we understand that tithing is the law of prosperity. If we want to become prosperous, we can't afford not to use it.

Volunteer work is also a form of tithing. Many who are not wage-earners find it beneficial to tithe time, talents or abilities. Those who tithe understand that tithing is not a payment, but a return, and that their tithe will return to them as a multiplied blessing. There are many many ways to tithe, all of them good. The surest way to increase your prosperity is to circulate it by tithing.

A short while after I had begun tithing my time and teaching ability at a school for special children, good things began to happen for me. My seminar and lecture engagements increased and Janey Jones (Editor) and I made rapid progress on the organization and completion of this book. It seemed that even the time that I was tithing was being returned two-fold. Best of all was the satisfaction I felt helping the children. That my time was being used in a constructive way was reward in itself.

Attract Prosperity when Paying Bills

When I pay my bills I use a green pen with green ink because I know the color green attracts money and success. After each check is written I hold it in my hand, bless it, and send it on its way believing more will come into my bank account. Bills must be paid so we might as well make it as pleasant an experience as we can. By releasing money with a blessing and with the faith that it will be replenished, you will attract more. Supply is waiting to be accepted by you.

In Summary

Remember, as Children of God we deserve happiness, health, and prosperity. Anything else is poor advertisement for our Father. We do not reflect an all-good and loving Father if we are poor and struggling. Prosperity befits a child of God. Supply is not limited. Our ability to receive is limited! Believe that you deserve good and you will receive your good. Work with the Law of the Mind - the law of attraction. Stop thinking lack and limitation and you'll stop attracting these conditions. Think SUP-PLY and ABUNDANCE in order to attract your needs, so that you can get on with you mission in life in peace.

CHAPTER VIII

Discovering and Achieving Goals

Discovering Goals

Some of us know what we DON'T want, but we don't know what we DO want. How do we discover our goals? What will give our life meaning? Since only we know our needs, and since we are our best source of information, we need to get in touch with the inner self for direction. During prayer and meditation ask, "What is my goal, my purpose in life? Then take time to listen.

Answers through Different Channels

Before I was led back to teaching (my niche), I searched "within" during prayer and meditation and asked repeatedly, "What is my niche? What should I be doing? What kind of job will give me the most satisfaction, the most fulliment?" After several days of earnestly asking and quietly listening, I received the answer in a most unexpected way. The leader of the Mind Development Seminar I attended asked if I would teach his seminar for him. He said, "Your life has changed since you've started using the information I teach, so you obviously understand it. You're an educator so you know the techniques of teaching, and you're bringing a lot of people to my classes." That was my answer. And that's how I found my niche - teaching and lecturing. If we seek answers from our inner self, we will get answers, IF we're listening.

The Holy Spirit speaks to us through whatever channels He can reach us - prayer, books, television, friends, newspapers, but we must listen. We must remain open-minded and receptive. Often we ask ourselves questions, but get caught up in distractions and trivia that block the channels through which our answers may come. Few of us enjoy quiet moments. We're afraid of the quiet. We think we need to be busy all the time. Learn to listen for messages wherever you are, whatever you are doing. You might be reading a newspaper and come across something that gives you an idea. THAT idea could be your answer. Or you might become aware of your answer while watching TV or in a conversation with a friend. Pay attention to that sudden flash of intuition, that "good idea" that "clicks" in such a way that we know when we have our answer. Learn to trust your intuition. This is your guidance from within. YOUR ANSWER IS TRYING TO GET TO YOU.

Achieving Goals

I suggest the following technique to achieve goals. With this technique you will utilize scientific, metaphysical and spiritual abilities. We are body, mind and soul and we must learn to develop and use all three energies if we are to progress towards self-realization. Once we have determined our goal, certain steps are necessary to attain it. Used correctly, the following is infallible.

1. BURNING DESIRE FOR YOUR GOAL. You must be sure that you really DESIRE the goal you say you want. This must be a "burning desire", not just lip service. Desire motivates. It produces feelings and emotions in the subconscious. Joseph Murphy, in the *Power of the Subconscious Mind,* explains that the subconscious mind is programmed by emotion - that emotion is the "vehicle" to the subconscious. When you feel your goal is right for you, that you deserve it, that you believe you can have it, you send a blueprint of this goal to your subconscious via emotion. Immediately your subconscious goes to work to bring into your experience whatever you are focusing on. You have put the Law of Attraction (what you think about, you bring about) into operation.

Remember, your subconscious cannot decide whether or not your goal is right or wrong for you. That decision must be made on the conscious level. Your subconscious is your "genie". Its nature and duty is to obey your command. Your "burning desire" gives this command.

2. BE SPECIFIC ABOUT YOUR GOAL. If you decide to build a house, you sit down and design every detail of that house. You leave nothing to chance. You make a specific blueprint to work from. Without the blueprint, the house would become a guessing game and you may end up frustrated and disappointed.

So, too, the subconscious must receive a blueprint from your conscious mind with complete details about your goals. The subconscious works best with a clear, detailed, specific picture.

3. WRITING GOALS AND USING PICTURES. I write my goals on a piece of paper and list every detail. Writing clarifies in my conscious mind exactly what I want and it gives my subconscious a concise plan to work from. BE SURE TO EXCLUDE ANY DETAIL YOU DON'T WANT. A friend wanted a Bonneville with a special interior - automatic windows, stereo, etc., but he didn't want a green car. Each day he visualized himself in his Bonneville and pictured the interior exactly as he wanted, then he added, "But not green". He got the Bonneville and it was green. The subconscious does not know NOT, so be sure you specify what you do want, not what you don't want.

If your goal is a material one find a colored picture of it and put it in your home where you can see it often. Or, you can carry a piece of paper with your goal written on it and look at it several times during the day. It is helpful to see a colored picture of your goal often or see it written because the subconscious works with images and with repetition. Each time you look at the picture or your written goal it will remind you of the commitment you have made to yourself and will impress the image upon your subconscious mind.

If your goal is peace of mind, get a photo of yourself in happier days and visualize your happy, peaceful expression. Put the photo where you can see it often. Seeing your goal often will make you begin to feel comfortable with the idea of having it.

Soon you will start to feel like this goal is really yours. When you reach this point, that you are comfortable with your goal, that it really is yours, the Law of Attraction begins to work and the subconscious will attract your goal to you.

Attract a Trip to Hawaii

A lady who had attended a seminar similar to the one I am teaching, wanted to take a trip to Hawaii and began programming her subconscious by visualizing a check made out to her for $2,000 thinking that would cover the cost. She visualized the check made out to her for that amount and visualized "God" on the signature line because she believed that God would provide it. Using the techniques she had learned - relaxation, visualization, repetition, emotion - she did receive the $2,000, but the money had to be spent on emergency medical bills. She complained to the seminar leader that it just didn't work. He told her she must be specific and said, "If you want to go to Hawaii, feel that sense of anticipation as you image yourself boarding the plane. Then see yourself getting off the plane in Hawaii, hear the welcoming "alohas" and smell the orchid leis being placed around your neck. Listen to the surf as you picture yourself walking on the beaches. Feel the warm sand and gentle breeze as you walk along the beaches. Enjoy the beauty of the tropical sunset. See, feel, and experience HAWAII, not $2,000."

She did as he suggested and some time later she met an elderly lady in the laundry room of her apartment complex. While waiting for their laundry to dry a converstaton about vacations came about. The older woman was looking for a companion to go with her to Hawaii, ALL EXPENSES PAID. Be specific. Work on your GOAL, not your plan.

4. KEEP YOUR GOAL A SECRET. Have you ever shared a goal with a "friend" and then went away feeling that the goal was impractical, absurd? Some people have a way of imposing their own limited feelings about themselves on to others. Because a "friend" thinks he can't succeed in obtaining the goal you've shared with him, he'll have you convinced you can't

either, that you are being unrealistic. "Be practical, " he'll tell you. What is practical? PRACTICAL IS WHAT YOU BELIEVE WILL WORK FOR YOU. Practical is what YOUR body, YOUR soul and YOUR mind believes it can achieve.

Hollywood with an 8¢ Stamp

Let me share with you the "impractical" way I got to Hollywood. After I left the convent, a friend suggested that the diary I had been keeping while I was probation officer my last year in the convent could be made into a movie. At the time, I simply shrugged my shoulders and forgot about it, but the seed had been planted.

About a year and a half later I remembered his idea. I had just moved to Denver and had no job, no friends, no money and was beginning to feel depression set in again, so I thought I'd better occupy my mind before I lost it again.

I wrote to publishing companies, the three major television networks and to some celebrities stating that I had a diary and that it might be made into a book or movie. Responses began coming, but they were all negative. "Thank you for your letter, but. . ." One day I read in Newsweek that Mr. Elton Rule had been elected President of ABC Television Network. I had nothing to lose but an 8¢ stamp (1972), so I sent him the same letter I'd sent to the others. About two weeks later I got a phone call from Maggie Duffy with ABC Movie of the Week Department in Los Angeles. She told me that the President of ABC had forwarded my letter from their New York office to her office and they would like to review some of my material to determine if it could be developed into a Movie of the Week. It was.

Now, had I told anyone that I was thinking of writing to the President of ABC television to buy my story for a movie, I'm sure they would have laughed at such naive impracticality. They would have given me the "practical" advice, "If you want to get to Hollywood, Duco, you'll need an agent and an attorney." I had neither of the above. I got to Hollywood on an 8¢ stamp! That was practical for me. Practical is what works for you. What

YOU believe can happen - no matter what appearances seem like.

So keep your goals a secret. Don't dissipate your energy in verbal expression and you won't risk being talked out of what you need or want by disbelievers.

5. BELIEVE YOUR GOAL IS POSSIBLE FOR YOU. Is your goal believable to you or is it a fun thought you play with in your mind? Are you serious about it? In order for you to attract your goal your self-image must be equal to it. You can't achieve a goal that is 6 feet tall if you self-image is 3 feet tall. You can't be successful if you see yourself as an unsuccessful person. You can't become rich if you feel guilty about money.

Self-Image

Why do we lack self-confidence, feel rejected, unworthy, unimportant? Psychologists tell us that approximately 80% of our physical and emotional personality was formed by the age of 6. We have been conditioned to believe that we have to struggle to achieve, that having money is evil. Someone else's false values and negative attitudes have been passed on to us. . .IMPOSED ON US. To overcome these attitudes our consciousness has to be raised to the Christ level. St. Paul admonishes us to "Put on the mind of Christ." The mind of Christ is the mind of faith and love, the two most powerful forces in the universe.

Jesus told us we all have a divine source of inner power when He told His apostles who were observing Him perform His miracles, "You can do these things, and GREATER." What did He mean? He meant we have the same power within us as He had within Himself. We are all children of God. Jesus BELIEVED He was and His works proved it. We don't believe this truth and our lives prove it. When we hear that we are the sons and daughters of God we think this is a poetic cliche'. This is TRUTH, not poetry!

If you have been the victim of a negative belief system - "I deserve punishment", "I'm not worth much," - use reverse thinking to correct it - "I CAN achieve, I AM itelligent, I AM happy. I have a Divine right to be at peace, healthy, prosperous and successful. My life is in Divine Order." Your subconscious works with repetition, so begin affirming positive statements about yourself repeatedly until you become convinced of the good you deserve.

All of us have a mental picture of ourselves. This mental picture is our self-image and determines whether we are successful or a failure, happy or miserable, healthy or sick, etc.

IF YOU DON'T LIKE THIS IMAGE CHANGE IT!

If you are in sales and want to succeed, but do poorly because of lack of self-confidence, look in the mirror and repeat, "I am a successful salesperson," until you feel comfortable with the idea of success. Then visualize yourself making successful calls to customers. See your satisfied customers thanking you for your fine product and good service as they give you additional orders. Keeping this image in your mind will psyche you up to approach clients and will give you a confident attitude of success which you will transmit to the client. Apply this technique to any profession to attain success and prosperity goals.

Small Goals - Stepping Stones to Larger Goals

For many of us small goals are more believable than larger goals and it may be helpful to start with smaller goals that will lead up to a major goal. For example you may want to receive a $5,000 monthly income, but because $5,000 per month is so unfamiliar to you it seems unbelievable - impossible - at first. If you are uncomfortable with this large an amount but do really desire it, begin by setting your goal for a $2,000 monthly income. Write $2,000 in green ink and put it where you will see it often enough for your mind to adjust to that amount. Visualize yourself making out monthly deposit slips for $2,000.

When you do this often enough, you become comfortable with the idea of $2,000 and you will attract it. Next, up your financial goal to $4,000 using the same technique. Then, finally $5,000. By increasing your goal gradually you build acceptance in the conscious and the subconscious mind and your major goal of $5,000 can become a reality.

It is also helpful to know what you will do with your financial increase when you receive it. Visualize yourself paying bills, traveling, making investments, buying gifts for friends, etc. And put as much emotion as possible into these daily visualizations. This makes the goal even more real to you, more meaningful and more believable.

You Don't Need a Plan Necessarily

Don't lose your desire for a particular goal because you can't think of any way to achieve it. A plan isn't absolutely necessary in achieving goals. All of us have had the experience of having childhood dreams come true very unexpectedly. Since first grade I've had a strong desire to go to Quebec. Three years ago I received an invitation to go there. No plan was involved; just an unexpected phone call inviting me. I rarely use plans to achieve my goals. My limited intelligence may be able to think of one or two ways to achieve them, and sometimes not at all, but Infinite Intelligence can think of many ways.

I enjoy conducting seminars for teachers but I feel uncomfortable about approaching schools on a business level. My first in-service training for educators came about by my being in the right place at the right time. While promoting a seminar in Huntingdon, Tennessee, I met with a group of teachers, one of whom was the Supervisor. She liked what I had to say and asked if I would be interested in conducting an in-service program for the faculty, contingent upon the District Superintendent's approval. However, the Superintendent was rarely in town and there seemed to be no way for him to meet or hear me to decide whether or not my material would be appropriate. A few days later, I was being interviewed on a Nashville TV show which Huntingdon received. At exactly the right moment one of the Huntingdon teachers turned on the TV in the teachers' lounge and saw me and ran to the Supervisor's office to tell her to watch me. The Superintendent just HAPPENED to be in town that day and both went to the teachers' lounge to hear my interview. The District Superintendent was interested in what I had to say and the next day I was notified that my in-service program had been approved.

A seminar I conducted at a local community college resulted in two more opportunities to work with teachers. The head-master of one private school and the founder of another private school attended and afterwards both men asked me to hold in-service workshops for their teachers.

No plans were initiated, but goals were achieved. I didn't lose my desire to do in-service because I dislike approaching schools with my ideas. There were other ways these goals could be achieved. Desire and faith made it possible. Once you have that burning desire for a goal you will see a series of events start to take place, one after another, and these events will lead you to your goal. You'll be at the right place at the right time. God in His Infinite Intelligence can think of a hundred ways to bring about your goals. We must work with Divine Intelligence and not put up any blocks of disbelief and doubt.

A New Watch without a Plan

A former student used techniques I teach and became the proud owner of a digital watch - without a plan. When she took her old watch to be repaired the repairman was alone in the shop and became very frustrated because he had several phone calls while trying to work on her watch. During one conversation he dropped her watch and broke it beyond repair. In utter frustration he told her to look in the case and pick out a watch. She pointed to the digital watch like she had been wanting and said, "I want this one but costs more than mine did." He said, "Take it!" Now if she had had a plan worked out on how to get a digital watch, I'm sure Plan A would not have been to have the repairman break her watch - but that's how it happened.

I don't propose to encourage laziness. I simply want to educate you about this power of faith and the power of our amazing mind. If you achieve goals by using plans, by all means continue using what works for you. Just know that you shouldn't stop desiring what you want because you can't imagine HOW you can achieve your goal. You can - if you believe it.

6. VISUALIZE YOUR GOAL. What you visualize, you create. Visualization or imaging is used by many athletes to improve their skills and athletic ability. Dr. Carl Simonton teaches his cancer patients to visualize themselves cured of cancer. Imaging techniques can be applied to any goal - material, spiritual, mental, physical. This is explained in detail in Chapter 5.

When you write your goal you achieve 12% communication with yourself. When you visualize your goal you achieve 88% with yourself, and by visualizing your goal you give your subconscious another specific blueprint to work with.

7. RELEASE YOUR GOAL. Once we discover our believable goal, have a burning desire for it and visualize it, the next most important step is to release it- let it go - and KNOW it will happen.

If we're uptight, anxious about reaching our goal, we delay it because of our anxiety. As difficult as it is sometimes, we must learn to relax. As long as we're anxious, it won't happen. We have to let it go. We all know of instances where a woman conceives a child after putting in for adoption (she's stopped worrying about it!). We all have friends who have met their future husband or wife after they've stopped searching and forgotten about wanting to get married.

Anxiety repels; relaxation attracts. Think of the times you've been so exhausted from struggling to achieve that you say, "I quit." You have no more energy to continue so you "give up" (release) and that's when you attract your goal into your experiences. Relax and let it come to you.

The fact that we ARE uptight and anxious about something shows that we lack faith and FAITH is THE ingredient to achieving. It is our magnet. The goal is there, but we attract it when we release it. To release is to have faith.

Rent Paid on Schedule

Several years ago I quit my "secure job" and began conducting seminars and lectures. This meant I had no regular salary to depend on each month and meeting bills was sometimes a challenge. One day, near rent time, I discovered I had only $2.00 in cash and $2.00 in my bank account which went towards the service charge. I was called downtown for an important meeting and went realizing that I might be spending my last $2.00 on parking instead of eating. But I released it and chose not to become anxious about something I could not control. The parking lot was full and I circled the block twice hoping to find a parking meter. There was one available the second time around and when I started to insert a coin I noticed there was an hour left on the machine. My meeting lasted longer than an hour and on my way downstairs I thought, "If I have a ticket, I'll have to borrow to eat AND to pay the ticket." When I got to my car there was no ticket and the meter still registered one hour. It was stuck! After giving God A+ for that, I told Him I was curious about how He would come up with $200 for rent that Saturday.

I had a seminar scheduled for Saturday but I wasn't sure I would have it because no one had pre-registered. At about 9 p.m. Friday a former student called to say she and three friends wanted to take the class.

On Saturday I earned $135 from tuition and selling tapes. When I returned home and opened my mail I found a check from someone who owed me money. After adding it all up, I deposited EXACTLY $200 in the night depository box. (If I'd had any smarts I would have focused on $2000. If it works for $200 it can work for $2,000, IF you believe it can!)

That incident made a believer of me. I knew I would always be taken care of and that I would always have what I need when I need it. Money comes in and goes out. It's always there when we need it. God is infinite and can think of unlimited ways for us to have what we need, no matter how bleak things look. There is no limit to God's power and goodness, but we must cooperate by using our mental resources, and faith.

Worrying doesn't improve any situation. It worsens the situation, adds stress to the body and blocks mental creativity and ability to arrive at a solution. Nothing but negativity is achieved by anxiety. Worry prevents us from reaching a higher mental frequency or level where we receive creative ideas and solutions to problems.

It's not easy not to worry when we find the rent due and no money in the bank. It's not easy, but it is ESSENTIAL not to worry. Anxiety doesn't put money in our bank account, FAITH DOES!

The last thing I do when I end my meditation on goal-setting is to send love and gratitude to the universe. Love is the highest vibration or force in the universe and this vibration SETS THINGS IN MOTION. I feel it makes our energy field called the aura, a stonger magnet. I simply say, "I send love and gratitude to the universe." Then I add, "Thank you, Father, for this or something better." The phrase, "or something better" leaves the channels open to Divine Wisdom to provide what is best for me.

Summary

After we have discovered our goal we must:
1. Have a burning desire to achieve it,
2. Be very specific,
3. Write our goal or post pictures of it,
4. Keep it a secret,
5. Believe in it,
6. Visualize it,
7. Release it to Divine Intelligence.

Of all these steps, most of us have most difficulty with relaxing and releasing. We're too impatient. We want it now, but maybe NOW is not the right time to have it. Let Divine Wisdom lead you to it at the right place and the right time.

And when you have received your good, don't feel guilty or unworthy. Make your good a permanent part of your life by accepting it wholeheartedly. Thank God for guidance in showing you how to use the laws of the mind and the law of life correctly that your "joy may be full."

CHAPTER IX

Color

Labortory tests and practical experience proves that there is energy in color which affects your health, comfort, happiness and safety. . .

Subject a person to a given color for as little as five minutes and his mental as well as his muscular activity changes. . .

Color Dynamics is in no way an experiment. Its principles have been widely tested in many fields with uniformly beneficial results.

Color Dynamics for the House,
Pittsburg, Pa., Pittsburgh Plate Glass, 1981.

Color Energy As a Science

When I began conducting my seminars in 1975 the most difficult subject matter for me to introduce was how color vibrations affect us. I knew that what I was teaching was based on scientific research, but at that time there was almost no public awareness of the subject. Today magazines, newspapers, radio and TV tell us about scientific discoveries that explain how color can influence our health, our productivity, our attitudes, etc. Now public awareness facilitates my instruction on the subject by confirming what I teach.

Color is energy; it is a vibration. Some blind people are able to discern a specific color by simply passing their hands over it. They feel a certain vibration and identify it as blue, red, orange.

When we see color, we see vibration. Color energy is visible. Perhaps this explains why we feel more energy on bright, sunny days than on overcast days.

Color and Vibration

Each color and shade has its own wave length and frequency and these different frequencies affect us in certain ways. In his book, *The Silent Pulse*, George Leonard states, "If you should glance for only a second at the yellow wing of a butterfly, the dye molecules in the retinas of your eyes will vibrate approximately 500 trillion times - more waves in that second than all the ocean waves that have beat on the shores of this planet for the past 10 million years. Were the butterfly blue or purple, the number waves would increase, since these colors vibrate faster."

In this chapter we will discuss the effect of the vibrations of the colors blue, yellow, red, orange, green, white and salmon-pink.

IT IS NOT ALWAYS NECESSARY TO WEAR OR DECORATE IN CERTAIN COLORS IN ORDER TO REAP THE BENEFITS OF THEIR ENERGY. VISUALIZING THESE COLORS SURROUNDING YOU HAS PROVEN EQUALLY EFFECTIVE.

Practical Applications of Color

Blue energy calms and soothes us - some mental institutions decorate in blue. It is also a spiritual vibration and some metaphysical churches choose it for this reason. Before I conduct a seminar or give a lecture I visualize myself in a bubble of blue energy to insure that I will be relaxed and calm while speaking to the group. I also recommend using this blue color imagery to teachers and parents who have difficulty in controlling children.

A recently divorced single parent had to manage her five young boys alone. She said their home was like a battlefield getting them off to school each morning. After she attended one of my seminars she decided to apply color principles to her rowdy crew. Each morning before commencing the daily battle, she lay quietly in her bed and visualized the boys standing before her in a huge bubble of radiating blue energy. Then she sent them thoughts of love and peace. She called me to say, "It works!" The boys' behavior had improved.

"A blue-painted schoolroom has been shown to calm down abnormally active shool children. And three painted 'pink rooms' in California's San Bernadino County Probation Department have repeatedly turned aggressive juveniles into docile lambs - in under ten minutes," says Clinical Services Division's director, Paul Boccumini, Ph.D. ("Pink's Hot Line to the Emotions" *Self* magazine, April, 1983.)

Yellow stimulates the intellect. Before taking tests or doing mental work you might visualize yellow energy surrounding you ... and wear yellow when taking exams.

Scientists have verified what man has known for a long time, that the energy from the color red stimulates the sex organs — hence expressions such as "the lady in red" or, "the red-light district." Vibrations from red make us energetic, too, so if you are hyperactive use red sparingly when you chose your clothes and decorate your home.

Red-orange stimulates the appetite. (Notice that fast-food chains use it.)

Green energy is a healing energy. On days when you're not feeling too well, sit and relax and visualize a green energy field or light around you, or wear green that day. Green is also the money color, so write your checks with green ink and visualize yourself in green to attract abundance into your life.

White is a protective energy which repeals negativity. I recommend to my students that they protect their families, pets, automobiles, homes and themselves by visualizing what they cherish in an energy field of white light. Develop the habit of surrounding yourself and your automobile in white light each time you get behind the wheel. This white energy field will protect you from accidents.

In metaphysical circles the white light is referred to as the "Christ Light of Protection." Those who attend seances are advised to protect themselves beforehand from negative influences by visualizing this Christ Light around them.

Salmon-Pink, the Miracle Color

The color energy that students write and call me about the most is salmon-pink, the color of the words on the cover of this book. Salmon-pink is the most forceful vibration you can experience. It is the vibration of universal love and has been used with the most remarkable results.

If you have difficulty in getting along with or communicating with any individual, simply visualize that person and yourself standing face to face in a bubble of salmon-pink energy and communicate love and peace to that person. Do this faithfully and I can promise you'll see an improvement in the relationship in less than a week.

My friend Helen had a good marriage but she wanted it to be better. She told me that she wished her husband would stop shutting her out and be more affectionate and communicative. Helen knew about salmon-pink but had used it only sporadically. I suggested that she make a CONCENTRATED effort to bring about the changes she desired. She called a few weeks later to report some very positive effects. She said she'd been using it every day and added, "The other night I wasn't able to sleep and decided to experiment seriously with color. I literally drenched my husband and me in salmon-pink. The next day he was noticeably happier, more affectionate and more communicative. He even complimented me on a new lavendar outfit, and lavendar is a color he'd never cared for previously!"

Women at the Tennessee State Prison tell me they get excellent results after visualizing salmon-pink around their instructors, other inmates and families and friends on the outside.

Office workers who have attended my seminars say they relax and visualize their employer, difficult co-workers and themselves in the salmon-pink energy field before leaving for work in order to improve office morale. One secretary told me she had changed the atmosphere of the whole office by "cleansing" it with salmon-pink.

She visualizes the sprinkling system "raining" pink energy throughout the entire office and has reported, "It's a pleasure now to go to work."

Another former student uses salmon-pink a little differently. She visualizes herself wrapped from head to foot in a salmon-pink "cloak of light" and explains the effect this way. "I'm working on my self-image — I know I have to learn to love myself more. When I put on the salmon-pink cloak of light I feel warmed, glowing, loved and loving ... I know all's right with the world. I love myself and can send out love and peace to everyone else."

On one of my assignments with a temporary service some years back, I was asked to work with a woman whom I found absolutely overbearing. The first day was awful. Before leaving for work the second morning I meditated and visualized her standing before me facing me, saturated in an energy field of salmon-pink light. I sent her love and peace. That afternoon she stopped typing, turned around, look at the two of us behind her and said, "You know, I feel like I'm glowing today!" Little did she know that she'd been enveloped early that morning in a salmon-pink glow. For her to actually FEEL it made me realize how powerful salmon-pink energy can be.

At the end of one of my seminars in Nashville, a young man came up to thank me and said that some of the information I'd lectured on was just what he needed to hear and would help him make a decision about a career change. He added that giving his resignation to his present employer would be very difficult. I simply shook his hand, thanked him for coming and said, "Good luck." A few weeks later he called me to say, "You can tell them all for me that it works!" Then he went on to tell me how he'd benefited from using the salmon-pink. He said that after making his decision to leave the company he'd have to muster up the nerve to inform his boss, a very difficult person for him to communicate with. "Finally," he said, "when I could think of nothing else to give me the courage I needed I decided to use the salmon-pink as you instructed." He added, "When you were lecturing I was sure you used it successfully, and that most of those attending would use it successfully, but I just couldn't picture myself visualizing salmon-pink around me and my employer. In my desperation I tried it before I left to present my resignation to my boss and I've never seen that man more mellow!"

A salesperson experimented for several days surrounding herself with salmon-pink energy before she called on her clients. On certain days she used it and on certain days she purposely did not use it. Her experiment showed that on the days she used the technique, attitudes towards her were pleasant and friendlier than usual. On the days she elected not to use it, attitudes were either indifferent or "the usual."

If you are nervous when asked to make an announcement, given an introduction or lecture before a group, meditate before leaving and visualize yourself confidently giving your presentation. In your mind see an energy field of white light around you to protect you from negative energy, then see blue energy to help you relax, and lastly see salmon-pink to facilitate communication. You will find the group will be interested and receptive to your presentation.

I have a young friend named Bob who lives about a thousand miles from my home. His mother called to say how disappointed and unhappy she was, for Bob had dropped out of school, was using drugs and was attracting undesirable friends. Each morning after that conversation, I lay in bed before getting up and visualized Bob in the salmon-pink energy field. Then I said to him mentally, "Bob, you are loved, you can return to school and enjoy it and graduate, and you are a productive individual." When I called his mother a few weeks later I learned he voluntarily returned to school, had a good part-time job on weekends to keep him busy, and has made a new friend who has had a positive influence on him.

The power of this salmon-pink vibration is limitless and distance makes no difference.

In Summary

The concept of color energy as a science may be new to you. The only way you can understand its effectiveness is to try it for yourself. You'll be convinced when you experience it personally. If you have an earnest desire to improve a relationship, environment or situation, put color energy to work for you.

Use soothing blue in stressful situations or to inspire confidence. Remember that yellow stimulates the intellect and red-orange stimulates the appetite and gives us energy ... Green is for healing and prosperity ... The white light protects and repels negativity ... and salmon-pink improves communication and all relationships.

CHAPTER X

Energy
Mental, Physical
and Spiritual

Interaction of Energies

We live in a "sea of energy" because the world we live in IS energy. Our physical body is like an electrical plant. Like everything else in the universe, it is made up of molecules and atoms (units of electricity). Because of this molecular energy everything vibrates. There is molecular movement in solids, liquids, and gases; therefore everything in the universe vibrates. Your skin vibrates, so do your eyes, your hair and the pages in this book — everything vibrates. Your brain gives off vibrations and energy and some individuals can move objects with this mind energy.

Our normal body temperature is proof that the body gives off energy (heat). In his book *Silent Pulse* George Leonard writes, "The human body, like the bodies of all living things, creates its electromagnetic field. Every cell contributes to this field, especially the active gland cells and the muscle cells, which produce relatively strong electrical currents upon each contraction. The nervous system is a network of unceasing electrical activity; the brain, an incredibly complex switchboard on which every light is twinkling, night and day. The electrical activity within the brain, as we have seen, is organized into pulsing waves which can be measured on the surface of the scalp, and which also can propagate out into space at the speed of light."

Spiritual healing demonstrates the power of spiritual energy. Christ was talking about this spiritual energy when He said, "Faith can move mountains." Faith is a spiritual FORCE and this is why in the chapter on goals I explained how faith works like a magnetic energy to attract our goals.

Since we are composed of body, mind and soul our physical, mental and spiritual energies are constantly interacting. One affects the other. When we dwell on fear and situations that cause anxiety, we transmit negative mental energy to the physical body and negative chemical changes take place in the body to cause ulcers, high blood pressure, headaches, etc. The interaction of energy can work to our advantage or disadvantage mentally and emotionally also. When we eat too much junk food, especially sugar, this causes negative physical changes which affect the function of the brain. Some people develop hypoglycemia, some children become hyperactive and show very little self control.

The Aura — An Energy Field

Each of us has an energy field surrounding us that is called an "aura." In this aura, "Energy frequency varies according to mood. Fear, anxiety, anger, or rage are identified as low-frequency energies. Wisdom, good will, optimism, creativity and love are among the high frequency energies. In all there are thought to be 49 frequency bands of energy. And the higher frequency you surround yourself with the better you will feel. A person's energy field can vary between 12 feet and 30 feet." ("Energy Dynamics" - *House and Gardens,* July 1978.)

The aura has been recorded by Kirlian photography as illustrated in photographs in *Psychic Discoveries Behind The Iron Curtain.*

Effects of Mental Energy upon Self

Because I am aware that these high frequencies and low frequencies in my aura are affected by my thoughts, I now make an effort to discipline my thinking. When I awaken in the morning, my first thoughts are, "I praise God, I bless this day, and I bless everyone I'll meet and every situation I'll encounter this day. My life is in Divine Order." I'm not trying for Sainthood in the Catholic Church by saying this. I'm using scientific information about the human aura and am "tuning in" to the highest frequencies surrounding me. I consider the human aura to be a magnet and when I operate on high frequencies in this aura I become a magnet to attract high frequency people and situations to me.

Most of us have had days when we woke up at a low ebb and the whole day followed a "low ebb pattern." The day was so bad you wondered why you even bothered to get out of bed. The next time this happens, "shake" the low frequencies you feel you're operating on and tune in to the higher invisible frequencies surrounding your physical body by thinking something happy, spiritual, pleasant, positive.

Because the human aura (invisible energy) extends 12-30 feet, others can be affected by it. Often we have heard people say, "I got negative vibes from him/her." We "feel" something from the other person. It's like "reading" his aura. This is why it's important to give attention to these feelings (vibes) we pick up, and to the information we're receiving.

How Our Mental Energy Affects Others

Now we know how our MENTAL ENERGY can affect our physical bodies, but can our thinking and feelings affect the body of ANOTHER person?

An apparently healthy baby vomited blood and died not long ago, 21 hours after its birth. A post-mortem revealed the baby had three peptic ulcers. Further investigation revealed the mother had been under extraordinary stress during the last three months of her pregnancy because of conflict with an alcoholic wife-battering husband.

Even more provocative than the case of the newborn with ulcers, Dr. Spezzano says, is the work of psychologist Denis H. Stott, who studied about 150 randomly selected Scottish mothers and their babies until the children reached age 4.

Stott found that when the parents were undergoing severe, continuing marital discord, the babies had a higher-than-normal chance of showing some neurological problems, behavior disturbances and slower-than-normal development. (*Psychology Today,* May, 1981.)

How Our Physical Energy Affects Others

Our physcial energy can also affect the physical body of another person. The growth of orphaned babies was stunted during World War II because the nurses did not have enough time to pick up and touch the infants as required for normal growth and development.

Touching and Physical Growth

In one of my seminars a nurse who worked in a hospital nursery in Kentucky told of an experiment with premature babies done by the nursery staff. Some of the cribs of the premies were tagged and some of the cribs were not. The infants in the tagged cribs were picked up and held more often in addition to the usual touching involved in feeding the babies and changing their diapers. The premies in the untagged cribs were touched only when they were fed or changed. The premies in both groups were weighed and measured daily. Those in the tagged cribs who got extra attention weighed more and grew longer than those in the untagged cribs.

Touching and Emotional Growth

Touching infants is also a MUST for their emotional health and development. "Scientific experiments suggest that all warm-blooded animals have an innate need to be touched and that among the effects of sensory deprivation are loss of appetite, slower than normal growth, a decline in intelligence, and abnormal behavior patterns. ("Have You Touched Anyone Lately?" — *Reader's Digest,* May, 1980)

"... More recent studies suggest that during formative periods of brain growth, certain kinds of sensory deprivation — such as lack of touching and rocking by the mother — result in incomplete or damaged development of the neuronal systems that control affection ... Since the same systems influence brain centers associated with violence, in a mutually inhibiting mechanism, the deprived infant may have difficulty controlling violent impulses as an adult." ("Alienation of Affection," *Psychology Today,* December, 1979)

ESP

Apart from perceiving information through our five senses we have a "sixth sense" called extrasensory perception (ESP). Some refer to information obtained through ESP, as psychic or intuitive information. Some skeptics refer to ESP as "witchcraft" or "works of Satan." Satan has nothing to do with this ability. It is a God-given GIFT to each of us — a tool or talent to be developed, not feared.

By developing this talent we will learn to make wiser judgements and more prudent decisions. By "tuning in" with ESP we link up with Infinite Wisdom and Intelligence. Some of us don't yet trust these feelings, this wise direction we attain through our extrasensory perception, because we confuse them with imagination. When you KNOW THAT YOU KNOW something, that's intuition, ESP, psychic ability. Call it what you will.

A friend told me that five minutes after leaving home to keep an appointment downtown, she had a STRONG FEELING she should return home. Following this impulse she turned the car around and drove back to her house. She found she had left the front door ajar — an invitation to burglary. She KNEW something was wrong at home, followed her "hunch" to return home to check it out, and possibly averted trouble.

Listen to your feelings, your "hunches" about a career, your child, a relationship, ideas to improve yourself, etc. Follow through with this guidance and you will become a person who makes intelligent decisions and appropriate judgements about people and situations.

Like a two-way radio the mind sends and receives messages. We've all experienced receiving a phone call or letter from a friend or relative and saying, "That's strange, I was just thinking about her." That friend either "received" the thought you had of her which reminded her to write to you, or the friend was thinking of you ("sending") while writing the letter and YOU received the message.

Some people are stronger receivers than they are senders. And some of us are on closer "wave lengths" with certain people, and experience a particularly strong sense of mental communication with them. I have such friends who will call me when I'm sending them the message to call.

When I moved to Tennessee I stayed with a former sixth grade student until I could find an apartment. This friend and I have strong ESP between us. He traveled all week and was home on weekends. About the middle of the week while washing my clothes I got the thought to wash his too. I gave it some consideration, because I didn't want to spoil him and have him depend on my doing his clothes for him on a regular basis. Furthermore, I suspected he was sending the suggestion via ESP. I decided, however, to do him the favor THIS TIME because I sensed he must have a busy schedule that coming weekend and wouldn't have much time to do his chores.

When he came home and went upstairs to his room to put his suitcase away I waited for his reaction to the folded clothes on his bed. As I expected, he ran down the steps and said, full of surprise, "You'll never believe this, but I kept saying all week, 'Joyce, wash my clothes. Joyce, wash my clothes'. " And I said, "YOU'LL never believe THIS, but I received your message, and it was MY DECISION to wash your clothes for you." I assured him he didn't have any power over me by using the power of ESP to speak to me, and emphasized again that it was MY choice to do him that favor.

When people underestimate the power of the mind over others they can be vulnerable to another's mental suggestions. Once you are aware of this power, you are in control. When you don't understand it you could be controlled. For example, after I decided to discontinue a relationship with someone, I had strong urges to call him. I KNEW he was sending me the suggestion to call. I received the message, but didn't have to pick up the phone. My awareness made me less vulnerable.

Knowing that we can transmit suggestions to others via ESP, should make us careful of the thoughts we project to others about the way we feel about them. If your child has been making F's on his report card in math, and surprises you and himself one day by making a "C" on a test your response might be a superficial pat on the head with, "That's great. Now I know you'll pass!" And after those words of encouragement you think, "Dummy! You just lucked out this time, you'll never understand math." Don't think for a moment that child is fooled by the pat on the head. He SENSES your FEELINGS and knows that you're not sincere. Children are very intuitive. ESP is strong in children until about 13 or 14 years of age.

If you are worried about attending a party you have been invited to because your spouse is an alcoholic and even though he/she has promised not to drink any more, you fear he/she might indulge at the party, my advice to you is not to entertain anxious thoughts about that by saying to yourself repeatedly, "I just know he/she will drink at that party." Remember, you can project the suggestion of drinking to that spouse by the way you THINK. The suggestion is more forceful to the degree of fear you feel. Instead know (without a doubt) that your spouse will enjoy orange juice, 7-up or whatever non-alcholic drink is available at the party. By doing this you transmit suggestions of sobriety to your spouse.

How Your Thinking Affects Your Surroundings

Can your thinking affect material objects? We know people who "hate" their automobiles and they have untold trouble with them and sometimes total them eventually, whereas people who love their car (old or new) are served well by that vehicle. Think about it.

Research shows the affect of thoughts upon plants. Two identical plants were placed in separate rooms. They were the same size, planted in identical pots, in identical soil, given the same amount of light, and watered on the same day with the exact amount of water. The only difference was that the person who watered the plants thought happy thoughts about Plant A while watering it, and thought negative thoughts while watering Plant B. Plant A grew stronger and taller than Plant B at the end of the experiment.

Techniques To Develop ESP

1. Call a friend to ask if he/she would experiment with ESP. Suggest that after you both hang up you will

both get to a relaxed state (alpha) and you will transmit a thought to him to receive in a relaxed state. Call your friend when you complete the experiment to ask what thoughts he received. If it doesn't work the first time, practice it again. This exercise will help you to become more intuitive.

2. Ask a friend or relative to sit in front of you. You have a deck of playing cards and will look at any card, then look into the eyes of your partner before you and THINK of that card. If the card is the ace of hearts, THINK "ace of hearts" while looking into the eyes of your partner. As you are sending the message, your partner will receive, if both of you are relaxed. After sufficient time is allowed ask your partner what the card is. Again, if it doesn't work the first time, practice it. Often partners are anxious to be right each time. As long as there is any degree of anxiety the mind cannot reach Alpha so it is necessary to emphasize relaxation. You will probably get a few wrong in the beginning, but as you learn to relax you will notice an increase in accuracy.

3. This exercise is done with 3 or more people. One person leaves the room while those remaining hide an object. After the object is hidden the person re-enters and everyone else closes their eyes, relaxes, and mentally directs the person who has just re-entered the room to find the hidden object. For example: If Jack has volunteered to leave, the group hides a ring under Alice's purse. Then the group directs Jack to find it when he re-enters the room by saying mentally, "Jack, look for the ring under Alice's purse." Again, it is necessary to be relaxed to do this successfully.

64

In Summary

As we discipline ourselves to develop our mental, physical and spiritual energies, we learn to take positive control over our lives. Now we have a choice. Why be down on ourselves and our loved ones when we can raise vibrations, both ours AND theirs and become happier and more productive? Why muddle through life when we can tune in to God's infinite wisdom and guidance? Be aware of and learn to use these energies. They are God-given gifts and they make our lives so much more interesting and enjoyable!

CHAPTER XI

Choices and Risks

A 45-year-old executive came to me for counseling. He had been with the same corporation for many years but was miserable in his position and afraid to leave. He doubted that he could find a comparable job, plus his corporation had excellent benefits and a fine retirement program to which he had contributed for many years. He was the sole breadwinner of the family and had heavy financial responsibilities. But each day he dreaded going to his office. I suggested he had the following choices:

1. He could change his attitude.
2. He could take the risk of leaving and finding something better.
3. He could stay and be miserable.
4. He could communicate his feelings to his superiors.

Let's study each of these choices.

1. CHANGE ATTITUDE. Our attitude is the only thing we're in control of. We rarely control things outside ourselves, but we can control what is inside of us — our attitude. Our attitude is the only thing we possess that no one can touch — unless we permit it. If we DO permit outside control, the effects can be devastating as some of us already know.

Sometimes we reap negative results from taking risks and sometimes positive results. What makes the difference? ATTITUDE! Attitude is a way of thinking or of looking at things based on a belief system. Failure is a result of negative faith. Success is the result of positive faith. Even an atheist can have faith. Faith is simply belief. Belief in self, your talents, a person, a situation, a project, etc. Faith is a magnet that transcends the "practical." Faith knows no barriers, no obstacles. Nothing can stop a believer.

Attitude is a matter of life or death, success or failure, happiness or misery. If we can control our attitude, we can cope with any situation. After I taught my class at the Women's State Prison in Nashville, one of the ladies wrote me a thank you note and added, "The one thing I got out of your seminar is that I realize they can confine my body, but not my mind." That's control. That's freedom. This inmate has learned how to be really free in a confined situation.

How can we change our attitude? Why are we miserable? What makes us unhappy? THE WAY WE THINK causes us to be unhappy. Our everyday thinking is a form of self-hypnosis. The subconscious works with repetition — repetitious thoughts, repetitious words. it also works with emotion and images. If we keep telling ourselves, "I hate this job," "I hate the boss," "This day is going to be miserable," we're setting ourselves up for these situations. The more we repeat our hates and focus on our miseries, the deeper these suggestions are impressed on the subconscious. We program ourselves with negatives. The subconscious mind has a blueprint of misery and goes to work automatically. Whatever program we put into the subconscious, we will see manifested in our everyday living.

How can we change this? Change the PROGRAM! Use the same power but reverse your thinking process. Bless the people you work with, send them love before leaving for work and during the day; say, "My life is in Divine Order; things are getting better; I'm happier in my work." With this attitude you will notice people and situations around you begin to improve. Not only will you change towards them, they will change towards you.

Once our lives start changing for the better and we begin to experience improved health, happiness and prosperity, our biggest problem is that we become impatient. When we start reversing our negative thinking, we want "instant change." We want it to hurry up and happen. But stop and think. Did the situation get like this overnight? Did it "hurry up and happen"? No! It developed over a long period of time, perhaps years. If we've put up with it this long, a few weeks or months of mental discipline can certainly be tolerated.

Remember the Law of Attraction — what you think about, you bring about. Evaluate some past situation and recall what your attitude and thoughts were at that exact point in your life. You'll see that your situation was a reflection of your thinking at that time.

2.   LEAVE AND FIND SOMETHING BETTER. Notice I say, "Find something better." So often we equate a risk with a negative outcome. Why is that? Maybe it's because we've programmed in a false idea of security. We've been taught to doubt ourselves, our self-esteem, so we fear taking risks, because we're afraid of losing our security. It is our so-called "security" that often limits us and keeps us from taking risks and developing the necessary potential to achieve our goals. "Security" holds us back and often locks us into a self-defeating, dead-end situation.

Because I now know how the mind works I would NEVER advise a person to take a risk of leaving his so-called secure position unless he KNEW he could make it. Unless you have confidence in yourself and the goodness of God and know that God can only will GOOD for you — then stay where you are. It goes right back to ATTITUDE. If you think you can, you're right. If you think you can't, you're also right.

Choices are often accompanied by risks. When I chose, at age 39, to be Joyce Duco rather than Sister Fabian, I realized that I would have to go where I could learn who Joyce Duco was and this meant leaving those who were still relating to me as Sister Fabian. This choice involved a great deal of risk because it meant leaving family, friends, my entire support system. I had no idea what I would find outside the security of convent life. And to add to the risk I chose to begin a new profession in a business world which I knew nothing about.

The only two professions I knew were teaching and counseling as a Probation Officer and I chose not to do either one. I chose to leave the security of the convent where I had never had to pay a bill, and go into a new world at an unpopular age to start an unfamiliar career. I was enthusiastic about the challenge. Had I not had that attitude, I would never have left.

People think my middle name is RISK. After one and a half years in Las Vegas, I felt I had to leave an emotional situation and moved to Denver where I didn't know a soul, but eventually managed to find a job with a large corporation. I finally realized that office work was not my forte and got into selling which eventually led me back to teaching and lecturing.

In each phase of my life, nun and probation officer in New Orleans, medical assistant in Las Vegas, office worker and saleswoman in Denver, I chose to take the risk of leaving rather than staying and being destroyed, and each risk (choice) led me closer to my niche. Unless we take risks, we may never know the good that is out there waiting for us.

If we could learn that security is believing that we will always have what we need when we need it! I have come to this conclusion because that's the way my life has gone. In these past ten years of adjusting and seeking, I've always had what I've needed. Not just on the material plane, but spiritually and mentally too. Just when I thought things were unbearable, something good happened because I kept expecting some good to happen.

3. STAY AND BE MISERABLE. Do some people choose this? Of course. You and I both know some that do exactly that! Why do they choose misery? Misery is different to different people. Some people choose to stay in what we consider a negative situation because they are actually more comfortable in this negative zone than they are in making an effort to change that situation. The effort to change is more uncomfortable to them than the "misery."

A former student who has been receiving treatment and counseling at Hotel Dieu pain unit in New Orleans has become aware that some people must be left with some pain. Not only can they live with it but they NEED it.

A recent article about Cher Bono told how bad her last marriage had been, and at the end of the article she was quoted as saying, "But I'm not stupid. I wouldn't have stayed if I wasn't getting something out of it." That's an honest statement! Some of us are staying in a negative situation because we're getting something out of it. We don't want to admit this to others and sometimes we try to hide it even from ourselves, but when we really get honest we see that we are playing the martyr. A martyr is comfortable in circumstances that others would find unbearable, and gets a certain satisfaction out of controlling others and making them unhappy. Again, misery means different things to different people.

I've been asked how a woman can survive living with an abusive husband. My question is, "Does a woman HAVE to live with an abusive husband?" If she has tried communicating to no avail and sees the situation worsening by hating more and more each day, how can they survive emotionally? This stress can only lead to mental and physical disorders.

If she does choose to continue living with him, she could ask herself, "What am I getting out of it?" She may enjoy seeing him remorseful, repentant, doting over her after he's been abusive, or she may NEED that punishment to satisfy some feeling of guilt. Perhaps she can cope with an occasional beating better than to risk trying to make it on her own. She may get satisfaction by giving him the silent treatment and playing the martyr. If she chooses to stay in such a negative environment she must be feeding off it in some way. NO ONE is obligated to be a doormat or to be destroyed by another person, and as I see it, she has an obligation to remove her children from such an environment so that they will not LEARN the abusive behavior and pass it on to THEIR children!

If things are so bad and we make no effort to change we are really saying one of two things:

1. We must be getting something out of it or we couldn't tolerate it.
2. Things are not as bad as we want others to believe.

When we really reach the breaking point we will make a decision to change things. When we've had enough we'll either change the situation or get out of it.

Maybe each of us has one person that we do too much for — we give them advice, money, our time, our energy. We're giving, giving, giving. Always solving their problems. Have you ever stopped to wonder if that person has ever experienced a feeling of accomplishment? Self worth? Strength? Maybe they haven't, because we do it all for them. And maybe any friction between us and that person comes out of that person's subconscious resentment for us because we are making them so dependent and weak. They may not tell us this, but they just MAY feel it.

I often hear men say that they're miserable at home — the marriage is over, no more love, no more affection. But they choose not to leave because the wife may "take them for everything." So they choose their money over a peaceful, loving existence that could be theirs if they left. There IS an alternative if they are willing to take the risk.

I feel most of our problems have to do with the people we permit in our lives. We don't have too much control over this on our jobs sometime, but we can control this in our personal lives. Why do we choose the people we find ourselves with? Do we need them? Do they need us? I'm not sure that a relationship based on dependence is a solid foundation, unless it's a mutual dependence, and the needs of both people are being satisfied and that BOTH are giving and receiving.

Sometimes we find ourselves with an ulcer and blame another person for our condition. If you feel this way, then you are admitting that person is controlling you. If that person IS the cause of the ulcer, why do you continue being a friend of this person? Communicate you feelings. If you don't, why not? Are you afraid they won't be your friend anymore? Thank God! If they leave you alone, you MIGHT get rid of your ulcer. Or are you afraid you won't be liked if you tell them how you feel? So what? As we mentioned before, the whole world didn't like Jesus Christ, and HE was perfect!

4. COMMUNICATE OUR FEELING. Why don't we communicate? What are we afraid of? I was blessed in the convent because we were taught to communicate and the importance of constructive criticism. Each of us was assigned a DEFI partner. We would observe each other and at the end of the month, or sooner if necessary, we would come together to give constructive criticism to each other. This would help us see how others observed us.

Sometimes we're the last to know how we come across as an

employee, employer, mother, wife, husband, friend, speaker, teacher. Constructive criticism can help us improve our relationship and develop professionally. Consider yourself lucky if you have a "defi partner" in your life. Caution: only mature persons should engage in constructive criticism. It should be with an objective and open-minded person who can guard against being too sensitive about what is being said. People don't WANT to hurt. Most of the time the hurt comes from the way we interpret or misinterpret what is said. Much hurt could be avoided if we could learn to communicate properly and then listen to get the real meaning of what is being said to us. Listen INTELLIGENTLY not EMO-TIONALLY.

Also, let us try to view a situation objectively. Have you ever gone into the office in the morning and said, "Good morning," with a smiling face and gotten a GRUNT for a response? Your first thought is usually, "What did I do to him?" We're so guilt pro-grammed that we seem always to turn to "What's wrong with me?" Nothing's wrong with you maybe. You happen to be the first per-son who came along for him to give vent to the anger he's feeling from some other source. Simply see that person as one who has a problem, but don't see YOU as being the problem all the time. Learn to deal with people and situations objectively and you will experience fewer hurts and disappointments.

Blessings in Disguise

See people as instruments in your life. Sometimes negative situations and people are necessary to make us take our next step toward growth. I used to hate one of my Mother Superiors in the convent. I blamed her for my struggling, sickness, depression, poverty after I left. I thought, "If it weren't for her I'd still be in my secure existence." But it was time to leave that secure existence and to take my next step. If it weren't for her I wouldn't be as ful-filled as I am today. Now I bless her. She was an instrument that made me decide "it's time for me to go now." She did me a favor. I now send her love.

Another person who did me a favor was the last man I worked for in a large corporation. It was such a bad situation that I decided to leave the company. Not only did I leave that office situation, but I promised myself never to work in an office again as a permanent occupation. He did me the greatest favor, because office work is not my niche. He too was an instrument. He made it so unbearable that I decided to leave the thing I disliked most.

If we take some risks and make the right choices, these will lead us to our niche. Each of us has a mission and until we discover this mission we are never completely fulfilled. I am happy now because I'm doing what I feel I am here to do — teach. Until each of us finds this mission, we'll never be satisfied with ourselves and if we're not good for ourselves we can't be good for anyone else.

So evaluate your situation and if you don't like it, ask yourself what your choices are. But don't ever say, "I don't have a choice. I don't have a way out." YOU DO. And if you stay in that negative situation, that's your choice.

CHAPTER XII

Understanding Negative People

All of us come in contact with negative people from time to time. Perhaps they are family members, perhaps co-workers, or possibly someone we have a close personal relationship with. Once we understand them, we CAN learn to deal with them.

Two Types of Negative People

I have categorized negative people into two groups. In Group A are the people who are negative either because they are not aware or because they don't know how to escape from their negative lifestyle. These people, once they become AWARE of their situation, really want out of all this misery — but they feel stuck. However, when they learn that change IS possible (through education, counseling, friends' examples, etc.), they make a concerted effort to change and usually do. I belonged to Group A eight years ago, but when I discovered how to change I disciplined myself and made POSITIVE LIVING A WAY OF LIFE.

The people who are chronically negative and enjoy every moment of it belong in Group B. For these people negativity is a way of life — a commitment. They have no intention of changing and God help us if we try to deprive them of their misery!

You NEVER ask them, "How are you?" unless you have the time and patience to listen to their boring monologue of physical complaints. Least of all do you ask, "How is everything?" This simple question, often innocently used as a greeting, can make you vow never to use it again. People in Group B will take this opportunity to fill you in and bore you with every negative person, place, and thing they have experienced since they last saw you.

Notice how they glow as they recount their "unhappy" life. They have a bad case of the "poor me's" and your attention and sympathy is the shot in the arm that keeps them going until the next person asks that uncalculated question.

Listen carefully as these people speak of their unhappiness. They would have you convinced that their lives are one tragedy after another. If so, it's because they have chosen tragedy as a lifestyle ... and they thrive on it. They need it. Somehow their natures require punishment, possibly to satisfy some conscious or unconscious guilt. Or suffering may be the way their need for attention is satisfied. Their self-image is so inferior they don't think they can attract attention and love from family and friends except through suffering and crisis.

The Need to be Needed

A close friend of mine has raised most of her grandchildren. There is one crisis after another in the children's lives as they grow older. . .problems with drugs, alcohol, undesirable companions brought into the home. She lends money that is never repaid. She supports them when they are unemployed. These young adults are constantly imposing on her and draining her. It wears me out just to THINK of her dilemmas, and I've had to stop putting myself in her place, as we've been taught to do. Her situation was beginning to depress me so much that I began, through necessity, to try to view her problems objectively. Then I started to realize that her nature is not my nature and because of this I wouldn't be able to tolerate her problems if they were mine. The disasters she has lived through would have sent me to a mental institution, yet SHE seems to survive and even thrive on them! Her need to be needed is greater than mine. She NEEDS these negative experiences, perhaps to satisfy some guilt, to control, to be loved, to attract sympathy. I only know that she has a built-in mechanism to handle stress that I don't have, and because of this I would have chosen to take different action with the grandchildren than she has.

This is why I don't recommend putting yourself in the other person's place all the time. What one person thrives on can be destructive for another. Psychological and physical needs differ in each individual, as does our threshold for pain and stress.

We Choose the Situations We Need

This was clearly demonstrated in a documentary about street people that was aired some time ago by one of the major networks. It showed scenes of people living in parks, in gutters, in sewers, sleeping under the cover of newspapers. "Street People" are individuals who literally live in the streets. While filming, one of the crew became attached to one of the little old street ladies and was sympathetic of her plight. Before he and the crew left New York this young man found an apartment for his new friend and filled her cupboard with food. A few weeks later he returned to New York, tried to visit her and found she had returned to the streets.

This true story helped me to realize that we don't always know what's best for the other person. The street lady chose the streets because she needed the streets. We might ask, "Is that normal?"

What is normal? Obviously for her, living in streets was "normal." For you and me it may be abnormal.

The nature of each of us is different and our needs differ. We can GIVE advice but we have no right to IMPOSE it because it may not suit the needs of that other person. I'm sure the kind young man was disappointed and confused that the little old street lady abandoned that apartment. While he thought she NEEDED shelter and food, she really NEEDED to be in the streets. Think about this the next time you try to tell someone what they need to do with their life. Most of the people we know are in situations they chose to be in.

The next time someone relates a stressful situation to you, just ask, "Why do you need it?" That will either shock them into a new way of looking at their problem, or offend them so much that they will never share their "suffering" with you again. Thank God!

If someone repeats the same problems day after day, month after month, even year after year, and nothing seems to change, they are telling you one of two things. Either the situation isn't as bad as they want you to believe, because if it were they couldn't survive, or if it is so bad and they've done nothing to change it, they need the suffering because they are getting something out of it. When we hurt enough we'll do something to change the situation.

I have one friend who complained incessantly about her failing marriage and abusive husband. One day, when she had enough, she left him and took nothing but the clothes on her back. She'd HAD ENOUGH and was ready to do something about it even if it meant leaving what she thought was security.

Christian Charity?

When I was teaching my philosophy about negative people in one of my seminars in Los Angeles, one of the students asked, "What about Christian charity?" I explained that it was my *Christian responsibility* to feel the way I do. We give our time, our advice, our energy or money to the same people over and over for long periods of time, and we see no improvement in their lives. Because we give so much to these negative people they have never experienced a feeling of accomplishment. Thanks to us they've never been motivated to achieve. They didn't have to. We did it all for them. I find this "kindness" UNCHRISTIAN and want no part of it.

These people we give to the most appreciate us the least. They lose respect for us and take us for granted as they watch us drain ourselves physically, psychologically, financially and emotionally, to give them. We are their doormats, and no one respects a doormat. Because of us they have developed into unmotivated self-centered individuals, and they hate us for it.

Discipline — An Effective Prescription

How is this remedied? By using discipline in our dealings with them. By refusing to bail them out of their financial and emotional dilemmas. Only when we stop taking care of them will they start taking responsibility for their own actions. Refuse to listen the next time they want to relate their same old tired tale of woe. And refuse to sympathize with them. Sympathy weakens people. It is not what they need. Clear, intelligent, disciplined advice is what can get them out of their doldrums IF they're ready to change. Also, in order to raise the vibrations of a negative person you might use the technique of salmon-pink energy suggested in the chapter on color energy.

Discipline is strength. Discipline is direction that says, "I care." I was an educator for 17 years in the parochial schools and I never EVER heard any student brag about an easy teacher or parent. They made jokes and laughed about how they "got away with murder," but they never bragged about them. The ones they DID brag about were the parents and teachers who were TOUGH — those who required discipline. They respected the tough ones, not the easy ones, not the doormats.

And let us stop trying to live through others, stop leading their lives for them. This only leads to stress and unhappiness on both sides.

We can't be good for others if we're not good for ourselves. We can't give what we don't have. If we want others to change for the better we need to give them a model to encourage their change. A model of strength and discipline. Sincere positive living will do more than a thousand words. As Ghandi said, "My life is my message."

CHAPTER XIII

Psychosomatic Health

"There is no illness of the body apart from the mind." (Socrates)

"Psychosomatic" comes from two words, "psyche" meaning mind and "soma" meaning body. "Psychosomatic" simply means mind and body working together. Unfortunately, the word psychosomatic has taken on a negative connotation and when most people use this term they are referring to the destructive way mind and body work together to produce disease, as in "psychosomatic illness." Those of us who understand how the mind works have learned that MIND AND BODY CAN ALSO WORK TOGETHER TO PRODUCE VERY POSITIVE RESULTS, thus we have learned that it is possible to attain PSYCHOSOMATIC HEALTH.

The body wills to be well. The body has unlimited capacity for health just as the mind has unlimited capacity for knowledge. The body also has ways of healing itself if we let it, and if we assist it with healthy thoughts.

When we become ill we often feel our bodies have betrayed us. It is not the body that is the traitor ... Our thinking (attitude) is the culprit. The body is the victim of diseased thoughts that are transmitted to it and the diseased thoughts cause negative chemical changes within the body, then the immune system weakens and disease sets in.

Unfortunately, many of us fear our bodies. We think of our bodies as unreliable machines that cannot be trusted to work properly. This constant fear of body malfunction is making the insurance companies wealthy. If we were more open to and educated about the influence the mind has over the body ... If we made a conscious effort to develop a proper mental attitude as a way of life, there would be far less need for health insurance. Our best possible health insurance is understanding how body and mind work together and developing a deeper faith so that we can handle stressful situations with a peaceful mind.

Participating in Our Healing

Some of us don't want to take an active part in our health because we lack the discipline to make the EFFORT REQUIRED to eliminate stress in our lives ... to ban harmful foods from our diet, to remain physically active, and develop a proper mental attitude to maintain health.

Not only do we NOT take an active part in our health, some of us are unwilling to participate in our healing when we become ill. We leave this to the doctor and to the medicine he prescribes.

After attending a workshop conducted by the Simontons in Texas, Dr. Bernard Siegel, assistant professor of surgery at Yale University Medical School planned a workshop for cancer patients to introduce some of the techniques he had learned to help them "improve the quality and extent of their lives." He mailed the information of the seminar to about 100 of his patients suffering from cancer. Expecting these 100 to inform their friends who also had cancer, he anticipated at least 500 responses. He received only 12!

What a lack of motivation! Life for some individuals is meaningless and unfulfilling. Many have no purpose in life, no direction. They feel useless, ineffective and unfulfilled. (Unfulfilled living also contributes to stress. Perhaps this is why there are so many suicides.)

Dr. Seigel has since found that:

- "About 15-20% of people who are seriously ill would perfer to die if given the opportunity.
- "50-60% of the patients are willing to get better SO LONG AS THE DOCTOR DOES THE WORK AND THE MEDICINE DOESN'T TASTE TOO BAD.

- "The final 15-20% say, 'I'll do anything I have to do to get well. Just show me'." (*New Woman,* November-December 1981 — "How to Get Your Body to Heal Itself Despite Great Odds")

How sad that so few people are motivated to live! Sad, too, is the lack of discipline in so many lives. Control and responsibility for something so vital as our own lives is apathetically handed over to another!

Norman Cousins is a remarkable example of one who loves life and is willing to do what it takes to prolong it and improve the quality ... Many of you have read about his incredible cure from a disease of the connective tissue, considered incurable. His physician told him he had "one chance in 500." He decided he would be that ONE who would make it.

After careful consideration and speculations about the cause of his illness and possible cure, Mr. Cousins formulated his own course of action for his recovery. His physician and friend, Dr. William Hitzig agreed to this plan, which included laughter, vitamin C and positive attitude. He watched humorous films, which made him laugh, and learned that laughter WAS indeed the best medicine. He discovered that ten minutes of hearty laughter gave him two hours of sleep without pain. He refused to believe his disease could not be cured and he welcomed the challenge to overcome his intolerable condition.

He goes on to say that people asked what he thought when told by the specialists that his disease was progressive and incurable. The answer was simple. "Since I didn't accept the verdict, I wasn't trapped in the cycle of fear, depression and panic that frequently accompanies a supposedly incurable illness. I was not unmindful of the seriousness of the problem or in a festive mood throughout. Being unable to move my body was all the evidence I needed that the specialists were dealing with real concerns. But deep down, I knew I had a good chance, and relished the idea of bucking the odds." (*New Woman,* March-April 1981 - "What I did When I Was Told My Disease Was Incurable")

Stress and Illness

The medical profession claims that up to 85% of the illnesses are stress-related or stress-induced. Chronic or prolonged stress, and negative emotions can cause negative chemical reactions to occur in the body, the immune system weakens and colds are contracted, ulcers are developed, and often the cancer cells that are ever-present in the body go out of control.

Tempo

Stress is different to different personalities. While some break down under the stress of meeting deadlines in high pressure jobs, others thrive on these conditions. What one person considers stressful, another may consider a welcome challenge. The threshold of stress differs in each individual as does the threshold of pain. It is important for each of us to know what our level of stress is and not go beyond it.

I meet a lot of people who are obviously in the wrong occupation, but insecurity and lack of self-confidence prohibits them from leaving and looking for a position more suitable to their tempo, more challenging and more fulfilling. Instead they choose to remain in the stressful, unsatisfying situation and thus become vulnerable to the development of stress-related illnesses.

Each of us operates at a certain tempo (the rate of speed at which we act or think). If Mr. Thomas is an executive who likes to take his time in making decisions and his secretary is one who is quick and likes to hurry with decisions so she can get on with the next project, she must either adjust to Mr. Thomas's slower tempo since he IS the boss, or the stress from NOT being able to adjust will soon take its toll on her health, and headaches, colds, backaches, ulcers, arthritic pain, etc., may occur.

When I left teaching and began office work I learned that the tempo of a teacher is very different than the tempo of an office worker — not better, DIFFERENT. As a teacher I had my own group, followed the same schedule daily, had an authoritative role and worked at my own pace. It was like having my own secure little world. The pace of office work almost did me in because it was incompatible with my tempo. I was running to get this file, hurrying to finish that project, typing a letter for one boss while another was standing over me waiting his turn. It was destructive to my health and I decided to leave that profession and all the benefits it provided — including health insurance. I concluded that if my job was causing me to use my "health benefits," I'd rather not have them.

Relaxation/Meditation Breaks

I hope we will see the day soon when ALL employees are given a choice of relaxation/meditation breaks or coffee breaks. The advantage of relaxation/meditation breaks is that after 5-15 minutes of mental and physical rejuvenation the employee returns to his tasks refreshed and relaxed, a more productive and creative employee and better able to cope with stress or the task at hand.

Visualization and Healing

I mentioned that when I realized my mind (attitude) was causing my illness, I concluded my mind could also stop and/or cure my illnesses. I used the same power, but in reverse. To me, psychosomatic health was more appealing than psychosomatic illness.

Often an illness or accident occurs after an emotional upset, an argument, or after a feeling of guilt sets in if you feel you've offended someone or after some traumatic event.

At the onset of a cold a few years back, I began reflecting on what emotional upset, if any, could have caused it. I recalled having unpleasant words with a friend, but at the time of the argument it seemed insignificant. I wondered if maybe subconsciously the argument had affected me more than I thought it had on the conscious level, and decided to use the following healing technique: I closed my eyes, relaxed and imagined a movie screen in my mind. On this screen I relived the unpleasant encounter exactly as I recalled it — unkind words, angry feelings — every detail. After recalling it as it occurred, I saw myself take a chalkboard eraser and erase that scene from my screen. In its place I visualized the encounter the way I would have wanted it to happen. I imagined us both enjoying a calm discussion about the problem and in a friendly way. Before the end of that day my symptoms of the cold were gone.

Instead of blocking the unhappiness or guilt I was feeling about the argument, I faced it by reliving it on my screen. By erasing it I removed the negative feeling and program from my mind so that it would no longer affect my body, and replaced it with pleasant thoughts for my subconscious to work with.

As this is new thinking to some of you, I only ask that you try it with an open mind. If negative emotion can cause illness, positive emotion can cure it.

Our Conditioning Attracts Illness

It disturbs me when I hear people say, "cancer runs in my family" or "I inherited my heart trouble" or "people in my family die young." Have you ever stopped to think that these ailments might "run in the family" because the inability to cope with stress, rejection, etc., "runs in the family?" As children we imitated attitudes and behavior of those in our immediate environment. If a parent worries a lot and has frequent moods of depression, disorders such as high-blood pressure, ulcers, etc., invariably develop. The inability to cope is influencing the child and the child will probably become an adult with that similar personality and prone to the same physical disorders.

So often sickness is a symptom. The real problem is some deep-laden guilt, rejection, hurt, burden that we've bottled up, not faced or failed to work through completely.

Other Psychological Causes of Illness

Aside from stress and feelings of guilt as causes of illness, some individuals may subconsciously attract illness for attention, control, convenience and as a means to escape duties and responsibilities. This is not to say that these people are not really physically ill. They are ill — and when we understand the power of the mind we understand why: we understand that their subconscious has received messages relating to their desires to be pampered, in control, or gaining attention, and it (the subconscious) had obediently provided opportunities for them to be pampered, in control and receiving attention via illness.

When I was an educator with the Sisters of St. Joseph, we were taught not to give in to ourselves. Because of this disciplined thinking I would never have asked to miss going to school unless I had a fever. There were days when I "dragged" myself to the classroom feeling like a limp dish rag, but because I had no temperature I couldn't justify staying home. On one occasion of feeling exhausted and in need of a rest from the children and classroom, I remembered thinking - with fervent desire - "I just WISH I could get away from the classroom for a while!" Before the week was out, I contracted the flu. My desire programmed my subconscious (as mentioned in Chapter 1) and my genie (subconscious) obeyed my command and provided the opportunity for me to miss class — fever and all. This was an illness of convenience — not chosen consciously, but on the subconscious level. I know some of you are smiling right now because you have experienced a similar verification of the power of the mind over the body. The mind is constantly working with the suggestions and feelings we are sending it. BE CAREFUL HOW YOU USE IT!

A student sat next to me at a lunch break at one of my seminars, and began telling me that since she had moved to Los Angeles she had gained weight which had made her husband unhappy; she was in and out of doctors' offices with different ailments and was seeing a professional counselor. At the end of the lunch she finally said, "When he (her husband) has enough, he'll let me go back to N.Y. where I want to be." This woman was actually willing to endure depression, overweight and physical pain to get her way! The games we play!

For some, illness becomes such an important and convenient crutch that they have no desire to be rid of it. Perhaps you have a friend/relative whose life is centered on his/her chronic pain. His business associates express their sympathy and concern, assist him as much as possible, and hold him in high regard for his dedication and his perfect attendance even on days his pain is at its peak. His family shelters him from unpleasant conversation about family problems so as not to upset him. Take his pain away and you take away the special attention he enjoys.

Some people need pain or chronic illness to avoid responsibilities and/or be excused from marital duties like helping with the children or avoiding having sex. If you know people like this, don't spend your energy on sympathy. Be kind to them, yes, but don't hurt for them or take on their pain. They are achieving something through their illness and they are not hurting as much as you when you put yourself in their place. Being drawn into their negativism only serves to destroy our own peace of mind.

When we have a healthy self-image we don't need illness to attract love and attention. A person with a healthy self-image knows that he is capable of giving love and worthy of receiving it by simply being who he is. Self-confidence and learning the art of communication can replace using illness for control and convenience.

In Summary

Psychosomatic health can be achieved by each of us when we are willing to make the effort. We know that psychosomatic health is possible because we have learned about the power of the mind and we have learned how body and mind can work harmoniously to achieve mental and physical health. Don't give energy and control to anything or anyone that can upset your body chemistry over a prolonged period of time.

Psychosomatic health is achieved by developing a strong faith to aid us in dealing with negative situations and people in such a way that we remain in control of our peace of mind. This is possible and it IS God's will. Physical and mental health is our divine right.

Suggestions to Achieve and Maintain Psychosomatic Health

- Remain physically and mentally active.
- Eat properly and moderately.
- Build self-esteem by knowing your worth as a child of God.
- Discover your purpose in life and possess a strong will to live.

- Set long-range goals.
- Overcome stress with faith in God's goodness and faith in yourself.
- Learn from the wisdom of past experiences that ALL THINGS ARE PASSING, and that what seemed to be a tragedy at one time, actually was a blessing in disguise.
- Enjoy your hours of work, or find work that you enjoy.
- Develop a proper mental attitude as A WAY OF LIFE.
- Be convinced that wherever you are, God is, and all is well.

CHAPTER XIV

How Children Are Affected by Their Environment

Psychologists tell us that at least 80% of our present emotional and physical personality was formed by the age of 6 (some say as young as 2). This means that during our formative years we were "conditioned" to positive or negative attitudes; to love, fear, hate, doubt; to feel self-confident or to lack self-esteem.

Because a young mind is like a sponge, the adults and older siblings in the family should be careful how young children are "programmed." Parents unknowingly program children with negative suggestions about health when they say, "Put your rubbers on because you will CATCH A COLD if you get your feet wet." These children get their feet wet when they swim and bathe don't they? Do they catch colds then? Most probably not, because they have not been "conditioned" to catch cold while having fun. What parents really want is for the child to put his rubbers on so he won't ruin his shoes. If this is so, then say THAT to the child. There's no need to threaten with sickness if he doesn't obey. Appeal to his sense of cooperation and obedience without threats. If this doesn't work, then use discipline. But appeal to their intelligence and sense of cooperation first.

Another negative suggestion often used is "Take your cough medicine or you're going to cough all night." We have just SUG-GESTED coughing all night, and if the child does, we have only ourselves to blame. Next time try, "Take your cough medicine so you can sleep all night." THE POWER OF SUGGESTION! Use it to BENEFIT others.

Learned Behavior

Before the age of 6, a child can only ABSORB ITS ENVIRON-MENT. He cannot discern whether what he absorbs is good or bad, because a child under age 6 has not yet reached the reasoning level of consciousness called Beta. Children are IMITATORS. Words and actions are new experiences for a child and they learn to act, speak and feel like those around them. Fortunately or unfortunately, adults are their only models.

Have you ever heard overweight people say they are heavy "because it runs in my family"? That's too easy. The problem is not someone else's genes as much as it that overweight persons learned habits of overeating from their parents!

During their childhood they saw full plates before them and before their parents. Children are imitators. They imitate your eating habits, your attitudes, your ability or inability to cope with stressful situations, your likes, dislikes, prejudices, manner of communicating with others, etc.

Negative behavior patterns are learned and are perpetuated with each generation if we are not careful. On a national TV talk show a young mother was being interviewed about her experiences with her former husband who inflicted physical abuse on her. She explained she tolerated it because she was afraid she wouldn't be able to support her two children alone if she divorced her husband. One day she saw her two children having an argument, and saw the little boy beating on his little sister who was curled in a fetal position with her hands over head and face, protecting herself. She realized her son was becoming abusive like his father and the daughter was reacting to it like her mother. LEARNED BEHAVIOR! This incident made her decide to leave her husband. She didn't want her two children growing up learning that physical abuse was a way of life.

Marriage and Parenting

Given the proper environment, training and opportunity, children can develop into incredible individuals. Human potential is limitless, as we have mentioned throughout this book. But if parents have not learned appropriate parenting skills from THEIR parents, they must learn it elsewhere. A knowledge of human psychology is essential to develop and perpetuate a stable marriage

and family life. Marriage is THE MOST IMPORTANT INSTITU-
TION IN OUR COUNTRY YET THE ONLY REQUIREMENT
TO ENTER IT IS A BLOOD TEST!

Hopefully the day will come when courses in marriage preparation will be another requirement to help couples learn to create a
strong family unit, rear well-adjusted children, and help them
develop the genius within. Too often emotionally and mentally immature couples marry, who lack the skills needed in parenting
children. The juvenile courts are full of the products of such a
union. These children are victims, not offenders.

Discipline

Oftentimes, reasonable discipline is what children actually cry
out for by their erratic behavior. Discipline is DIRECTION. A lack
of it leaves kids floundering during their formative years of development. Discipline is STRENGTH. A lack of it spells lack of responsibility and weakness on behalf of the adult. Kids see weak discipli-
narians as doormats and NO ONE respects a doormat. They lose
respect because they see the adults depriving themselves of peace
and happiness to satisfy the kid's demands and whims.

When Phyllis and David York, developers of the TOUGH-
LOVE program, tightened the reins and enforced disciplinary actions on their troublesome teenagers, their behavior improved.
Toughlove is a nation-wide support group for parents, to help
parents to take charge of their families again. They learn to set
limits, take action, support one another and work with community
agencies to effect healthy changes in their families and within the
community. Toughlove has helped thousands of parents stop the
self-destructive behavior of their children and build cooperation
and stability in the family unit.

CAUTION: IF YOU SUSPECT DRUGS OR ALCOHOL
SEEK HELP IMMEDIATELY THROUGH A REHABILITATION
CENTER OR ALCOHOLICS ANONYMOUS OR NARCOTICS
ANONYMOUS. Chemically dependent kids (those dependent on
drugs or alcohol) NEED MORE HELP THAN THE FAMILY CAN
PROVIDE. Ten to fifteen percent of our adolescents are

chemically dependent! The yellow pages will list drug and alcohol treatment centers and Alcoholics Anomymous and Narcotics Anonymous groups in your area. Utilize them.

Communication

One technique I found effective in dealing with unruly kids in the classroom was to talk with these children quietly after school when the classroom was empty and our tempers had subsided. I'd ask, "Why have I asked you to stay after school?" After the reason for the disciplinary action was clear, the next question was, "If you were in my place and had my responsibility what action would you take?" Interestingly enough the punishment they suggested was often more severe than what I intended to mete out. But the real accomplishment resulting from those two questions was COMMUNICATION. We both had the opportunity to explain ourselves to each other in a calm and objective manner. The student was able to give me details — what he really meant by his action and why he did it (jealousy, attention, anger, etc.). I was able to show him how I perceived his behavior, how it might have affected the class, and also to suggest other ways of coping with or communicating his feelings.

After our mature and informative communiation I told him what disciplinary measures I'd decided upon and he left with a better understanding of why he was being disciplined. No grudge, no hostility. Because we communicated without emotions flaring, we were able to view the situation objectively and clearly.

I might suggest that parents confront their children with the same questions. The attitude of both at the time of the confrontation is important. Wait until atmosphere and tempers have cooled. (Anger begets anger.)

As respect builds between parent and child through better communication, the incidence of poor behavior will decrease.

Boys at a Canadian reform school were asked to write some guidelines for parents. This was their advice:

- Bug us a little. Be strict and consistent in dishing out discipline. Show us who's boss. It gives us a feeling of security to know we've got some strong support.

- Call our bluff. Don't be wishy-washy and don't be intimidated by our threats to drop out of school or leave home. If you collapse, we will know we beat you down, and we will not be happy about the "victory." Kids don't want everything they ask for. ("Families Forum," *Families magazine,* June 1982.)

Pre-Natal Experiences

Communication is the secret to mature and healthy relationships of all kinds — interfamily relationships especially. But this kind of communication doesn't begin when the child is 8 or 10 or 15. It begins at birth, when the child is able to sense and absorb the feelings of the parents.

As mentioned earlier, some researchers are now learning that we were influenced by our enviornment BEFORE BIRTH. That the fetus is affected by the parents' emotions, thoughts, even the sounds in its environment. A device called a hydrophone can be inserted into the uterus a half hour before delivery to record conversation and music played in the room.

"Now that we know sounds penetrate the uterus and that the fetus is a discriminating listener, shouldn't we ask what effect violent TV programs might have on it? How about loud arguments between husbands and wives?"

"For years the idea of prenatal impressions was laughed at as fanciful folklore. But tests now show that the mother's anxiety increases the baby's heart rate."

"In one experiment pregnant women who smoked were deprived of cigarettes for 24 hours. The next day they were offered cigarettes again and fetal hearts started beating faster EVEN BEFORE THEIR MOTHERS COULD LIGHT UP." ("Life Before Birth," *Science Digest,* December 1982)

Would that all expectant parents could understand the influence they have on their unborn child! And would that mothers and fathers of the unborn could develop a closer and more loving relationship for each other and express verbally and with deep feeling their loving anticipation for the unborn TO the unborn! The result would be a society peopled with individuals who have healthy self-images and self-esteem.

Making Up for Past Mistakes

Some of us responsible for the development of children, have made mistakes in good faith simply because we were not aware of what researchers of human behavior are now learning.

Some students of my workshops worry that they are responsible for the unhappiness, lack of self-confidence, poor self-image and lack of love their children are currently experiencing, and they ask how to correct this now, after the children are older. I suggest that they mentally ask the wronged persons forgiveness and send love and peace. This is the technique I use to right the wrongs I was unwittingly guilty of while I worked for 17 years as an educator molding young minds. I sit quietly, breathing deeply until I feel myself slip into Alpha. Then I visualize the person I might have wronged, in the salmon-pink energy field. I send that person love and peace and ask forgiveness. I have found this to be a most forceful and effective method of healing.

Children and TV

I have read numerous articles reporting that Saturday morning cartoons are too violent for children, especially preschoolers, to view. A steady diet of this kind of violence influences the behavior of preschoolers by making them less imaginative at play and more aggressive (fighting and kicking). This shouldn't surprise us since while watching these cartoons children view at least 25 violent acts per hour.

Reports show also that a steady diet of violent TV programming can affect the behavior of adolescents in school and of adults in their relationship with their family.

As mentioned in the chapter on the subconscious, our subconscious mind is programmed by repetition. What we hear and say repeatedly is a form of self-hypnosis. It stands to reason then that if we are exposed to hours of viewing TV each week, what we see and hear repeatedly will surely influence our attitude and behavior.

Can the viewing of repeated acts of violence on TV affect the mental health of a family? Think about it.

Food Children Eat

When I was principal of a grade school in 1963 we had two little hyperactive first graders on tranquilizers. From reports I get from students who attend my seminars, the number is increasing. The main culprit — too much sugar in the diet. It affects the functioning of the brain as well as other major organs in the body and robs the body of necessary vitamins and minerals.

A 12 year old boy had experienced recurring bad dreams, lack of self-control, and chronic fatigue and stomach pains since age 10. He had become increasingly combative, and repeatedly started arguments at home and at school. When his pediatrician could find nothing medically wrong with him and suspected a poor diet, he recommended a nutritional evaluation. The results showed that his diet consisted of "empty calories" such as sugar cereals, chocolate milk, pie, soft drinks, cookies. Urine and blood tests indicated several areas of deficiency, particularly in B Vitamins.

The child's parents were advised, "to eliminate candy, doughnuts, and ice cream from his diet, and to add more vitamin- and mineral-rich foods such as fruit, hard-boiled eggs, and whole grain products. They also gave him B-vitamin supplement pills daily."

Within 3 weeks "new tests showed he no longer suffered from chronic nutritional inadequacies we had found earlier. His school work improved and his random aggressiveness virtually disappeared." ("The Junk-Food Syndrome," *Psychology Today,* January, 1982).

One way to begin eliminating sugar from a child's diet is to stop giving sweets to children as a reward. Find a nutritional and satisfying alternative.

Adding Positive Mental Attitude Courses to School Curriculum

As mentioned in Chapter 2, some school systems are incorporating the study of death into their curriculum. The students are taught attitudes about death, they visit mortuaries and witness embalming. Since death is certain for all of us perhaps this is appropriate preparation for the inevitable. But how many schools teach LIFE? Life is NOW. It is DAILY. Life must deal with inevitables too: disappointment, stressful situations, negative people. How prepared are we to deal with these conditions? Incorporating Positive Mental Attitude courses into the school curriculum, perhaps through science, psychology or health courses, will not only prepare our young people to cope but will ultimately reduce or prevent negative mental attitudes from developing.

School administrators and those who design curricula could greatly improve the mental health and quality of life in our society by introducing and making mandatory courses in the development of PMA to help our young people build self-confidence and self-esteem. A student can earn many degrees in engineering but if he lacks self-confidence he will not become a successful engineer. However, if he feels good about himself he'll succeed at anything he does. Teaching PMA would certainly be a bonus for our whole country.

Communicating While Children Sleep

During sleep our conscious mind shuts down and we go into different levels of subconsciousness. When our children are at these subconscious levels we can communicate with them mentally even though we can't seem to reach them through verbal communication during their waking hours.

For example, the parent of a six-year-old who wet the bed every night used mind-to-mind communication to help her child sleep dry. Following my suggestion she waited until her daughter had been asleep for about thirty minutes. At that time she went to a quiet room and got to a mentally relaxed state of mind (Alpha) by using the method explained in the chapter on meditation. In Alpha, she mentally pictured the child standing before her and said to her, "If you feel like going to the bathroom during the night, simply get up and go. Then come back and enjoy a nice dry bed." The mother called me the day after she'd used this technique to say that for the first time in her life her daughter had not wet her bed.

I mentioned this success story in a class and a couple attending called to report THEIR results using the same method. They both had gone home after my class anxious to apply the technique on their children, ages 4 and 6. The mother mentally communicated with the six-year-old and the father mentally communicated with the four-year-old. At the time they called, neither child had wet the bed for the entire week.

This method can be applied to any situation where there is a lack of verbal communication with children or with adults.

If you have a teenager who needs direction, but is hard to reach because of peer pressure, "growing pains," ego, inferiority complex, etc., "talk" to him while he sleeps and say the positive things then that you have difficulty communicating verbally.

While he is asleep, choose a quiet room to relax and meditate. (You can do this even if you are on a business trip in another state or country. Time and space make no difference at the sub-conscious levels of the mind.) When you feel relaxed, visualize your teenager standing before you and say to him non-verbally what you would like to say verbally.

Example:

> "John, you are loved and important. You are full of confidence and you have a healthy self-image. You are making reputable, mature friends with whom you can share constructive activities. Your life is useful and fulfilling and you are happy."

Then visualize that child in a bubble of salmon-pink and send love and peace to him. You'll be amazed at the healthy change you'll begin to see SOON.

To improve your relationship with your spouse wait until he or she is asleep and visualize you both standing together surrounded by salmon-pink energy, communicating in a loving, understanding way. Then send love and peace to your spouse.

This non-verbal, mind-to-mind communication works, but you'll never know it unless you try it!

As I've emphasized earlier, mind-to-mind communication is powerful and anyone using it should have enough sense of responsibility to use it only for the good of others. If it is used in a destructive way, to gain control or to harm others, remember "AS YOU SOW, SO SHALL YOU REAP." If we do anyone an injustice the universe owes us one.

Mental Depression and Suicide

As an educator from 1951-1968 I witnessed many social changes that influenced children's and adults' life styles and behavior. Some parents were ill-equipped to handle these changes in their own lives, and they weren't very effective in directing children and helping them cope with change. Today, in the 1980's it's worse.

We live faster and harder because we're not sure about tomorrow. Our impatience to achieve NOW is creating stress which in turn is causing serious illness and strained relationships. We don't take time to sit and talk about what's happening with our lives. If we can't deal with it or understand it we escape it with superficial relationships, with drugs, with alcohol or with suicide.

Millions of people in our society are depressed, but my main concern is depression among our young. According to the National Center for Health statistics say more than 5600 young men and women under age 25 took their lives in 1981. Why are so many of our kids depressed? I believe kids have more pressures than adults. You might argue that adults have as many. If they (adults) do, remember, they are more mature and have more experience and knowledge, and have more control over their lives than young people have, thus they are better equipped to handle these pressures than kids are. Young people don't have these advantages. Youth is still "wobbly" and not certain about life. Security is important to them and that security is knowing that their parents love them and won't abandon them, no matter what. They need this assurance throughout all stages of development.

Because of increased divorces more children are experiencing physical and emotional privation at an early age. Peer groups just might be a substitute for "security" they don't get from their parents.

In our fast and furious pace we don't take time to develop meaningful relationships — the source of our support system. And because of this pace and its demands, young people live harder and faster than previous generations. The pace takes its toll on their mental and physical health.

Summary

This has been a difficult chapter to write because the subject is broad and complicated; therefore, I've decided to sum it up with a few suggestions which I hope will help you as parents in dealing with and understanding your children better.

Negatives

- Don't nag kids to do better in school. Only an unkind parent demands more when it's obvious the child is doing his best. Your pressure is defeating them.
- Don't nag them about not being able to make up their mind about a profession TODAY! The working/business world is new to them. I can relate to their indecisiveness. I went through it at age 39. Many of us know WHAT WE DON'T WANT, and we don't know WHAT WE DO WANT. Taking time to experience different professions can be helpful.

98

There's something wrong if this goes on forever, of course, but reasonable "trying out" can be advantageous in the long run.

- Don't nag them to become a chemist, doctor, athlete, astronaut to make YOU LOOK GOOD AS A PARENT. Don't use them as a status symbol. Sometimes parents inflict more unnecessary pressure on their children than do their peers. This is when communication between child and parent ceases because the child feels, "it's no use." So they begin communicating to a peer group about you and your demands.
- Don't become competitive with your children. That's immature and it shows.

Notice I used the word "nag." Giving advice and suggestions is one thing, harping on kids to do OUR WILL is something else. Too many parents want to fulfill their dreams through their children. UNFAIR! The nature, needs and desires of their children may be different than those of the parents, and it is destructive to pressure a child to embrace a profession or mate in life like dad or mom always wanted. If you want something so badly, YOU GO OUT AND ACHIEVE IT, and don't impose this kind of pressure on your child.

Positives
- Do encourage them to discuss anything with you and let them know you will respect their confidence and not make light of it.
- Do build their self-esteem. The cure for peer pressure is a strong self-image. They won't need the approval of their friends if they know their own importance (not overrated ego), and they won't succumb to the pressures to be accepted.
- Do answer their questions honestly and sufficiently so that they won't have to go to undersirable sources to get answers.
- Do be an example of faith in the goodness and the love of

God. They need a model to learn from.
- Do seek outside help if you suspect your child is chemically dependent.
- Do let your children know you love them for what they are and not for what they accomplish.

Hats off to the young adults and to the parents of those who emerge into adulthood with firm moral and spiritual values and whose lives reflect these beliefs. You're stronger than you think and are to be congratulated!